Africa's Forgotten Empires

From the Dawn of Egyptian Civilization to the Modern Age

By Saeger Godson

Copyright 2013 by Saeger N. Godson

No part of the publication may be reproduced, stored in or introduced into a retrieval system, or transmitted, in any form, or by any means (electronic, mechanical, photocopying, recording, or otherwise), without prior permission of the author. Requests for permission should be directed to SaegerGodson@yahoo.com

ISBN-13: 978-1481920575
ISBN-10:   148192057X

Preface

Two years ago, I began the biggest project of my life. Ever since I can remember, I have loved to study history. For me, history is the greatest story that mankind could write. It is an ongoing saga that has no end, and we are all given a chance to play a part in it. Most importantly, history graphically depicts mankind's journey. This journey is made up of man's great triumphs and great tragedies. It is through history that I gain a healthier perspective of the world I live in. Studying history is my most cherished and addictive hobby. Many of my causal conversations digress into monologues about my latest historical interests. Indeed, my infatuation with history is so great that my parents suggested I write a book. At fourteen, I decided to give it shot.

The timing was perfect because at that age I was engrossed in African history. In my view, African history has largely been ignored by historians and the world. Many people think of Africa as a continent of natural wonders that is alien to civilization. Growing up, I studied world history and was greatly dismayed that my history textbook had so little to say about African history. This led me on a journey to rediscover African history on my own. As I searched, I discovered that Africa did in fact have indigenous civilizations. These civilizations spawned throughout the history of mankind. Civilizations such as Kush, Egypt, Ghana, and Great Zimbabwe defy the notion that Africa has no history. As I discovered more about Africa's past, I felt compelled to write a book about it. I noticed that there are already many scholarly books written about African history, such as Basil Davidson's *Lost Cities of Africa* or Robert B. Edgerton's *Fall of the Asante Empire*; however, there are not many books on African history that appeal to the general public. As a result, I decided to write a condensed book on African civilizations.

For the next year and a half, I spent many days researching and writing about African civilizations. I was amazed to discover that Africa has a history as dynamic as Europe, Asia, and the Americas. Africans built powerful empires, vast cities, magnificent palaces, and even prestigious universities and libraries. There were great African rulers, such as Mansa Musa, Thutmose III, and Taharqa, who were among the most powerful men of their day. After my rough draft was complete, I moved on to my next task: editing. I am forever grateful to my grandmother and my parents for their assistance in that area. Finally, working at our local park district, I successfully generated the money to publish my book.

It still amazes me how little the world knows about African history. I hope my book can help dispel this apathy. I am writing this book in order to reach the general public with the truth of African history so they may know that Africa also has played a key role in mankind's never-ending story: history.

Contents

Introduction	1
Chapter 1: North Africa	7
Ancient Egypt	8
The Kingdom of Kush	24
Carthage	28
The Moorish Empire	37
Chapter 2: East Africa	47
Ethiopia	49
The Nubian Kingdoms	58
The Swahili States	66
Chapter 3: West Africa	73
The Empire of Ancient Ghana	76
The Mali Empire	82
The Songhay Empire	90
Kanem-Bornu	97
The Asante Empire	103
Chapter 4: South Africa	113
The Munhumutapa Empire	113
Epilogue: The Legacy of African Civilization	117
Bibliography	123

Introduction

When one thinks of Africa what comes to mind? Jungles, savannas, or how about lions and elephants? When one thinks of Africa, one thinks of natural wonders and beauty, but what about its history? Many people have thought of Africa as the mysterious "Dark Continent"; however, most of these same people are familiar with civilizations like Egypt and Carthage, yet these civilizations only represent a portion of Africa. Let's look at some geography facts. Africa is the second largest continent in the world. In fact Africa is over three times the size of Europe. Just looking at the history of the northern coast would be incomplete. In order to understand the true history of Africa, we must study the entire continent.

For years, many people in the Western world have been led to believe that Africa has no history (or at least none worth mentioning). However, this is one of the most terrible misconceptions in the world today. Africa is rich with history. Unfortunately many people believe Africa had no significant history until the African slave trade only about five hundred years ago. Many people are led to believe that pre-colonial Africa was inhabited by barbaric tribes fighting among themselves and lacking civilization. Let me quote a statement found in an old world history of textbook of mine:

"At the dawn of the 19th century, Africa the Dark Continent, remained by and large an unexplored mystery. But it was no mystery that Africa possessed a wealth of natural resources. The nations of Europe saw Africa as a vast treasure chest waiting to be opened. Though it is the second largest continent Africa has only recently begun to play a role in international affairs."

This statement is completely false. Many African nations played key roles in international affairs for thousands of years. For example, the nations of Egypt, Carthage, the Swahili Confederation, and the Mali Empire all played major roles in international affairs during their time. To be honest, many of these nations were involved in international affairs before Europe. When Britain was inhabited by Celtic tribesmen, Egypt led the world in civilization. Just look in the Bible: Egypt played many important roles in early biblical history, not just in Exodus, but all throughout the time of the kingdoms of Judah and Israel. The power of the African nation of Carthage was felt all over the Mediterranean before Rome even existed. Their merchant fleets sailed all over the earth, sending trading expeditions to distant lands. During the medieval era while Europe was in its age of darkness and unending warfare, the kings of Mali were believed to be some of the richest men on the earth. And the cities of the Swahili Confederation were the important trading ports in the Indian Ocean. Therefore, Africa has been involved in international affairs and commerce for over three thousand years. Consequently, that textbook statement has no creditability and should be modified.

The fact of the matter is that most of the history that people are aware of today is observed though the eyes of Europeans. But there is a major problem with this Eurocentric view. Europe did not start playing a critical role in world history until the rise of the Greeks around 600 BC. According to some Christian historians, the earth is about six thousand years old. [2] If so, that means if we only look at the history of Europe, we are missing more than half of world history! Just imagine all of the history we are overlooking. Europe did not play a significant role in human history until the latter half of mankind's existence.

So, in reality, our view of world history needs to change so we can fully understand it. Otherwise, we end up having to ignore many nations and empires that have also contributed to the world we live in today.

But before that, let us go back to the beginning of African history. African history starts shortly after the Tower of Babel, when God, the creator of all things, commanded the people of the earth to be fruitful and multiply and to spread out all over the world. But the people did not listen and decided to build a city and a tower to reach the heavens. At that time, all of the people in the earth spoke one language, and there were no barriers between them. When God saw what they were doing, he decided to give the people different languages, but then the people were not able to cooperate with one another; thus, they never finished the Tower of Babel. The people left the Tower of Babel, which was in the land of Shinar in the Middle East, and migrated all over the world. Some of the people crossed over the Sinai Peninsula into Africa. Biblical historians believe that three of the four sons of Ham—Mizraim, Put, and Cush—migrated to Africa after the Tower of Babel. Their other brother Canaan settled in the Land of Canaan, which is now called Israel.

There has been a long controversy about the origin of the peoples who first settled in Africa. To start there are some of the West who still believe people of African descent are bound to a curse called The Curse of Ham. They base this theory on an event in the Bible involving Noah and his son

Ham in Genesis 9:20-25, which reads:

"20 Noah, a man of the soil, proceeded to plant a vineyard. 21 When he drank some of its wine, he became drunk and lay uncovered inside his tent. 22 Ham, the father of Canaan, saw his father's nakedness and told his two brothers outside. 23 But Shem and Japheth took a garment and laid it across their shoulders; then they walked in backward and covered their father's nakedness. Their faces were turned the other way so that they would not see their father's nakedness. 24 When Noah awoke from his wine and found out what his youngest son had done to him, 25 he said, 'Cursed be Canaan! The lowest of slaves will he be to his brothers.'"

Now what they, for some reason, miss is the fact that Noah said, "Cursed be Canaan," not Ham. Canaan was only one of Ham's four sons. Ham's other sons, Mizraim, Kush, and Put, migrated to Africa. Canaan migrated to the Land of Canaan in the Middle East in modern day Palestine. So, the sons of Canaan are not even Africans to start with. This, of course, proves that the Curse of Ham theory is nothing more than an attempt to make people of African descent believe that it was God's destiny for their lives to be inferior. When we read the truth, we understand that God blessed the sons of Ham as well as all of mankind. It was from Mizraim, Put, and Kush that the first Africans were born, and as the families grew larger, they began to disperse all over the continent.

So now that we have gone over the beginnings of African history, we can begin our study of the peoples and civilizations that were founded there. Unfortunately, most books on African history focus on the events that occurred during and after European colonialism. This book goes back as far as the founding of Ancient Egypt over four thousand years ago.

Because of Africa's massive size, we will divide the continent into four main parts. First, we will briefly overview North African history. Second, we will move on to East African history and discover its fascinating nations and cultures. Next, we will study the history of West Africa and learn of its mighty empires and peoples. Later, we will go through the history of South Africa and the civilizations that sprang up there. Finally, the importance of studying history is to learn from the successes and mistakes of the people before us, and we will do that by summarizing all of the history we've studied to find a message for the future.

(Abu Simbel, Egypt)

Chapter 1: North Africa

The history of North Africa begins with Mizraim, one of the three brothers who crossed over the Sinai Peninsula into Africa after the Tower of Babel. It was from Mizraim that one of the first African empires came to being in Egypt. Many know a little history of Egypt and have seen pictures of the Pyramids, so this might be a review. Now, let's take a closer look at the history of Egypt.

Ancient Egypt

The nation of Egypt emerged on the banks of the River Nile in 3200 BC and was among the first civilizations on earth. Starting at Lake Victoria in modern day Kenya, the Nile flows 4,184 miles north to the Nile valley in Egypt and empties into the Mediterranean Sea, making it the longest river on earth. The Nile River is sometimes called the lifeline of Egypt. This is true because if the Nile did not exist, the land of Egypt would be a desert like most of northern Africa. However, the Nile was like a gift to the people who settled there. In fact, the Nile was such an important life source that the Egyptian calendar was based on the flooding cycles of the river.

The Egyptians began to settle in the Nile Valley around 3200 BC. Soon there were villages and later cities rising all over the valley. Egyptian history is divided into three main time periods: the Old Kingdom, the Middle Kingdom, and the New Kingdom. Between each kingdom there was a period of political unrest. Originally, Egypt was divided between the Upper and Lower Kingdoms. However, in 2700 BC the two kingdoms were unified under King Mena. Ruling from the new capital of Memphis, Mena is believed to have reigned for sixty-two years and was Egypt's first pharaoh.

As Egypt continued to prosper, its people began to make great technological advances. In modern times, archeologists have found skeletons of Egyptians whose heads were cut open then sowed back together. Mind you, these are not cuts from an ax or weapon of some kind; these cuts resemble a surgical operation. In the New York Academy of Medicine, there is an ancient Egyptian text now called The Edwin Smith Papyrus. This text has forty-eight accounts of bone surgery and external pathology. This implies that the Egyptians were some of the first civilizations to pioneer the science of surgery.[3] There were also advancements in engineering. During the fourth dynasty, the Egyptians built the Helwan Dam. The dam consisted of stone, rubble, and other walling. When complete the dam was 321 feet wide at the bottom and 184 feet wide at the top. As many as five hundred workmen were employed in the construction, and it was a great demonstration of the Egyptian hydrological knowledge.

Besides advancements in technology, Egypt began to engage in commerce in the Mediterranean Sea. Surplus grain production was traded in the Middle East, and the Egyptians imported lumber and olive oil. Egypt obtained gold, tin, lead, and flint from trade in the Red Sea. With the wealth they acquired from commerce, they built beautiful cities, palaces, and other monuments. Trade brought great power to Egypt, which soon became one of the mightiest nations of its time.

As the Egyptian kingdom continued to expand, the Egyptians soon engaged in wars with the Nubian peoples to the south and the Libyans in the east. Pharaoh Sneferu of the fourth dynasty is recorded to a have gone to war with Nubia and took seven thousand prisoners as well as capturing two hundred thousand cattle. Later he marched on Libya and captured eleven thousand prisoners and 13,100 livestock. These raids increased the Egyptian treasury in addition to tribute and taxation.

Also in the fourth dynasty, there were the first records of pyramid construction. The Pyramids were tombs constructed for the pharaohs. Building the Pyramids was a daunting task; it took tens of thousands of workers and many years to complete. There has been great controversy on whether the Pyramids were built by slave labor or by skilled workers. It has been a popular notion that the Egyptians used several thousand slaves to build the Pyramids, but leading archaeologists and historians have found that they were probably built by skilled employed workers. Evidence of this is from archaeologist Mark Lehner who stated in an article by *Harvard Magazine* titled "Who Built the Pyramids?":

"This notion of a vast slave class in Egypt originated in Judeo-Christian tradition and has been popularized by Hollywood productions like Cecil B. De Mille's The Ten Commandments, in which a captive people labor in the scorching sun beneath the whips of pharaoh's overseers. But graffiti from inside the Giza monuments themselves have long suggested something very different."

The idea that the Pyramids were built by slaves originated from the book of Exodus. In Exodus, the Hebrew people were subjected to harsh labor by the Egyptians. Now most biblical historians believe that the events in Exodus took place during either the late Middle Kingdom or the early New Kingdom period around 1500 or 1200 BC. However, the majority of the Pyramids were built in the Old Kingdom period around 2500 BC. Therefore, the construction of the Pyramids and the enslavement of the Hebrews were almost a thousand years apart.

This might be hard to grasp, but let's think about it for a second. Remember the Egyptian calendar is based on the flooding cycles of the Nile. The cycles are divided into three seasons. First, there was Akhet, the flooding season from June to September. During this season the Nile River overflowed and flooded the farmland along the blanks. Consequently, with their farmland flooded, the common people were free to engage in societal tasks, such as building the Pyramids. The second season was Peret, sowing time, from July through August. During this time the Nile receded and left fertile soil behind, so from October to February the Egyptians planted crops. The last season, Shemu, was the harvest time, from March to May. At this time the Egyptians harvested their crops. Each month consisted of thirty days plus five festival days totaling to 365 days. So during the flooding season, the Egyptians had four months every year to devote to building great structures like the Great Sphinx and the Pyramids. The construction of the Pyramids required much more than just raw man power. The Egyptians were among the first people to study geometry and mathematics. In conclusion, the Pyramids and other great Egyptian structures are symbols of advanced architecture, great knowledge in mathematics, and societal man power, not slavery and oppression.

Today the Pyramids are listed as one of the seven wonders of the ancient world. Out these seven wonders, the Pyramids are the only wonders that still stand today. The greatest of the Pyramids was the Great Pyramid of Giza constructed by Pharaoh Khufu around 2560 BC. In summary, the Pyramids are an excellent example of Egypt's technological advancement and power.

As Egypt continued to flourish, it became a world power whose influence could be felt from Canaan all the way to Nubia in central Africa. Pharaoh Pepi II led Egypt in many conquests in southern Nubia. Also noteworthy is the fact that Pepi II reigned for ninety-four years, making him one of the longest ruling monarchs in history. However, the power of the pharaohs was slowly diminishing. By the sixth dynasty, the nomarchs (local governors) had become more powerful, and they significantly undermined the pharaoh's authority. Unfortunately, toward the end of Pepi II's rein, the nomarchs and the priests gained greater power. The pharaohs after him failed to maintain their authority, and without strong leadership, the Old Kingdom collapsed around 2200 BC. The fall of the Old Kingdom meant a halt in progress, and Egypt fell into a struggle for survival.

After the fall of the Old Kingdom, Egypt was divided by turmoil. Historians call this time the First Intermediate Period. During this time the nomarchs warred with each other for the basic means to survive. Egypt was in constant warfare between the provinces, and technological and societal progress halted. Also during this time, people from the Middle East (called Asiatics by the Egyptians) invaded the Lower Kingdom. Several short-lived dynasties rose and fell during the chaos. Egypt remained in political unrest for a little more than a hundred years.

Around 2080 BC Egypt was reunited by Mentuhotep II, following the defeat of the Heracleopolitans (one of the Asiatic peoples who invaded during the First Intermediate Period.). This marked the beginning of the Middle Kingdom. With Egypt reunited, the land once again prospered. The pharaohs again erected lavish temples and palaces. In Nubia, pharaoh Mentuhotep IV constructed fortresses whose size and complexity was comparable to castles in Middle Age Europe. Also, Egypt established control over gold mines in Nubia and the turquoise and copper mines east of the delta in the north.

During the Middle Kingdom, the reign of Pharaoh Senusret II stands out as one of most eventful times. During his reign he improved irrigation in other regions by building several dams and canals. Besides that he is also credited for constructing the city of Kahun, which was one of the first examples of a planned city in history. Under the reign of Pharaoh Senusret III, Egyptian armies seized Palestine, which spread Egyptian culture throughout the Middle East. There were also great developments in art during his reign.

The last great pharaoh of the Middle Kingdom was Amenemhet III. He is credited for building two important pyramids. However, after Amenemhet III, the power of the pharaohs continued to decline. The last ruler of the dynasty was Queen Sobekneferu, and the end of her reign marked the end of the Middle Kingdom. Once again Egypt fell into chaos, the Nubians regained independence, and Asiatic peoples from the east took control over the northern delta.

During the Second Intermediate Period, Egypt was once again divided into weak provinces under the rule of nomarchs. The eastern delta was overrun by nomadic tribes from the Middle East. The increasing numbers of Asiatic slaves and freemen who had been brought to Egypt during the Middle Kingdom had great influence in the coming years. Soon the delta became an independent nation ruled by Asian kings, who some historians believe to be the first non-black rulers in Africa.

These peoples ruled Egypt for about two hundred years.

However, around the seventeenth century BC, Egypt was conquered by the Hyksos. The Hyksos are believed to be of western Semitic ancestry. The invasion of Egypt by the Hyksos was a quick conquest. One account by Manetho (an Egyptian historian and priest from Sebennytos) stated:

"During the reign of Tutimaos a blast of God smote us, and unexpectedly from the regions of the East, invaders of obscure race marched in confidence of victory against our land. By main force they easily seized it without striking a blow; and having overpowered the rulers of the land they then burned our cities ruthlessly, razed to the ground the temples of the gods, and treated all the natives with a cruel hostility, massacring some and leading into slavery the wives and children of others...Finally, they appointed as king one of their number whose name was Salitis. He had his seat in Memphis, levying tribute from upper Egypt. In the Saite nome he founded a city...and called it Avaris".

Form the city of Avaris, the Hyksos controlled the trade routes leading to the Middle East. They also made alliances with the kingdom of Kush to secure trade routes with southern borders. The Hyksos ruled northern Egypt, while surviving Egyptians remained in southern Egypt. In the early sixteenth century BC, native Egyptians, led by Seqenenre Tao II, launched a bloody campaign to retake northern Egypt. The Hyksos, however, had the latest weaponry, including chariots, giving them a formidable advantage. Despite these disadvantages, the Egyptians fought for the next thirty years. During this war, Seqenenre Tao II perished in combat. He was succeeded by Kamose, who continued the rebellion. Under Kamose the Egyptians pushed the Hyksos back to the delta. Kamose unfortunately died before the Hyksos were completely defeated, but he did turn the tide of the war.

Under Ahmose I the Egyptians drove the Hyksos out of Egypt and founded a new dynasty, which marked the birth of the New Kingdom. Ahmose I, then pharaoh, set out to build an Egyptian empire. He first invaded Canaan and gained access to several key copper mines in the region. He then conquered the Kushite territory of Wawat in the south, gaining control of the gold mines in the region. Ahmose I also limited the nomarchs' control, strengthening the pharaoh's power.

The Hyksos invasion had a decisive impact on Egypt. Before the invasion, Egypt had never had to fear of a major foreign invasion. One of main reasons of this was that Egypt was almost completely protected by natural barriers. To the north and east were mountains and deserts, which discouraged invasion from the Middle East. To the west and the south was the Sahara Desert. The only other way to invade Egypt was to sail down the Nile River into Egypt. However, before reaching Egypt, there were several parts in the Nile where it became extremely shallow (known as *cataracts*), which prevented ships from sailing straight into Egypt from the south.

Consequently, Egypt never had to focus that extensively on its army. Although Egypt flourished socially and culturally, it fell behind in weapons development. The Hyksos invasion proved that Egypt had fallen far behind in war technology. However, during the Hyksos-Egyptian war, the Egyptians gradually acquired the Hyksos' weaponry. The Egyptians replaced their stone clubs with bronze axes and swords, and they replaced slingshots with composite bows. The Egyptians also mastered the art of chariot warfare. The chariot was the equivalent of a battle tank in ancient times. With these new weapons, the Egyptian army was prepared to establish an empire.

After the conquest of the kingdom of Kush by Pharaoh Thutmose I, Egypt stretched from the Euphrates River in the Middle East to the Land of Kush in the south. Egypt's next great ruler was Queen Hatshepsut. Hatshepsut revived the trade routes that had been disrupted under the Hyksos. She also made several maritime voyages to Somalia establishing trade sites there. Another interesting aspect of her reign was that she proclaimed herself pharaoh, a title usually given only to male rulers. Yet, she ruled Egypt with power and masterful diplomacy. Many great temples and buildings were erected during her reign. Hatshepsut's reign was relatively peaceful.

Pharaoh Thutmose III ascended to the throne after Hatshepsut. During the reign of Thutmose III, Egypt faced threats to its interests in the lands near the Euphrates (Syria). Several Asian kings allied together in an attempt to drive out the Egyptians. Thutmose III mobilized an army and marched against the Asian kings. Thutmose III's troops engaged the Asian forces at the Plain of Esdraelon, and the Battle of Megiddo ensued. Thutmose III decisively crushed the rebellion and continued his campaign into North Syria. After several more militarily campaigns, Thutmose III reestablished control over Syria. Thutmose III applied the same tactics against the Kushites in the south. During the reign of Pharaoh Thutmose III, the Egyptian empire reached its farthest extent, truly another golden age in Egyptian history.

After the establishment of the empire, Egypt continued to prosper both socially and politically. Merchants from around the known world were drawn to Egypt. Resources like iron, copper, fine linen, ivory, wine, and many others flowed into Egypt, enriching the empire. Egypt was now in its golden age.

The next pharaoh to be mentioned in Egypt's history is Amenhotep IV, who many historians note as a religious reformer. He later changed his name to Akhenaten, meaning "He who is of service to Aten." Akhenaten enforced monotheism in Egypt, which had been more polytheistic prior to his reign. To firmly entrench monotheism in Egypt, he built new temples for his god Aten, the god of the sun. He also appointed all new officials and priests, many of whom were of a lower class or even of foreign peoples. Lastly, he built a new capital, Akhenaten, named after himself. By around 1492 BC, Akhenaten had established his new religion, which ushered in a revolution in traditional art. However, the empire was facing serious threats in Asia and was gradually losing its foothold on its Asian territories.

Akhenaten was succeeded by Tutankhamun. Pharaoh Tutankhamun's chief priest worked to undo Akhenaten's religious reform, and the city of Waset regained its position as the capital city. However, Pharaoh Tutankhamun failed to suppress the Asian revolts. In time, Tutankhamun was succeeded by Seti. Pharaoh Seti led several campaigns against revolts in Asia and Nubia. However, the Hittite Empire in Asia Minor threatened Egypt's power in the Middle East. Like Egypt, the Hittite Empire was expanding its influence in the Middle East, and war was inevitable. Seti's son, Ramses II, led an army of around twenty thousand soldiers against King Muwatalli II of the Hittites. The outcome of the Battle of Kadesh is a little uncertain; some historians believe that the Hittites defeated Rameses II, yet, according to the Egyptians, Rameses II returned to Egypt claiming to be victorious. However, most historians believe that after a brief skirmish both armies returned to their nations proclaiming victory. What we do know is that both armies sustained heavy casualties and that both empires seemed to decline in power in the following years, so it would seem that the end result of the Battle of Kadesh was a stalemate. As for Egypt, it began to lose its control over its territory in Asia, and from that point forward, the Egyptian Empire was in decline.

As Egypt began to decline, it weathered many revolts in Nubia and Asia, followed by an attempted invasion by the Libyans and their Mediterranean allies. Despite this turmoil there was one last great achievement. During the reign of Rameses III, there were documents that imply that the Egyptians made maritime voyages to the Americas. It is certainly interesting that in parts of modern day Mexico there are large temples that resemble the Pyramids in Egypt. The many pyramids built by the ancient Mayans also suggest possible Egyptian influence in the Americas. If true, then the Egyptians could have possibly visited Central America about three thousand years before Columbus.

However, back in Egypt, the Sea Peoples of the Mediterranean threatened to invade Egypt. Even though Rameses III did defeat the Sea Peoples, Egypt struggled with internal corruption. Famine and crime were so abundant that many of the Pyramids were plundered of their treasures by criminals. Rameses III is remembered as the last great pharaoh of the New Kingdom; unfortunately, later pharaohs were weak, and the government was increasingly corrupt. The last pharaoh of the kingdom was Rameses XI, who was so weak that the High Priest of Amun Ra became ruler of southern Egypt. By the end of Rameses

XI's rein, Egypt collapsed, and the ruler of Kush declared independence from Egypt, which cut off Egypt's gold supply. The end of Rameses XI's rein (1070 BC) marked not only the end of the dynasty and the New Kingdom but also the end of the golden age of Ancient Egypt.

Egypt was then divided into small independent states that warred with each other frequently. Egypt was later invaded by people of Libyan descent. During this time, Egypt enjoyed a little unity under the rule of Libyan pharaohs, but soon the Kushites invaded and established the mighty twenty-fifth dynasty. The Kushites ruled Egypt until 671 BC when the Assyrians invaded and made Egypt one of their territories. About one hundred years later in 525 BC, Egypt was invaded by the Persians. The Persians ruled Egypt until they were defeated by Alexander the Great in 332 BC. The Greeks ruled Egypt for the next three hundred years. However, the Greeks in Egypt were defeated by the Romans at the Battle of Actium in 31 BC. The Roman Empire ruled Egypt until around 500 AD. Egypt was then ruled by the Byzantine Empire until 639 AD when the Arabs invaded. The Arabs controlled Egypt until they were defeated by the Ottoman Empire in 1517. The Ottomans ruled Egypt until the collapse of the Ottoman Empire in 1922. Egypt was then placed under British control until it declared its independence in 1953 and has remained independent to the present.

Today Egypt is remembered as one of the greatest

civilizations on earth and continues to amaze both historians and archaeologists with its glorious wonder and mystery. Egypt was extremely advanced in architecture, language, and society and no doubt had a great influence on Western culture. However, in the world today, there is a great controversy concerning the Egyptians' racial identity. For some reason many people in the Western world believe that the Egyptians were a white or Caucasian people. This is false. The depictions of Egyptian people on temple walls clearly contradict this idea. By observing these depictions, it becomes clear that the Egyptians were of black African descent. The face of the Great Sphinx, for example, has clear black African features, not Greek or Arab. Many other Egyptian statues also have Negro features as well. Also, Egypt is a hot and sunny climate, thus making it difficult in early times for people with little melanin to inhabit such lands.

Of course, it is important to note that as times changed the land of Egypt was invaded by many different peoples. Some of these invaders were other African peoples, such as the Libyans and the Kushites, while others were Asian and later European, like the Assyrians and Arabs as well as the Greeks and Romans. However, it must be pointed out that these later peoples did not build the Pyramids or invent hieroglyphics, for it was after the fall of the Egyptian nation that these foreign peoples invaded and now make up most of the population in the land.

Now, some historians would argue that Egyptians saw themselves as a different people or people group. The Egyptians may have thought of themselves as a different people from their other African neighbors, but that was more of a sense of national identity than racial identity. In the same way that the Greeks saw themselves differently from the Celtics and other European peoples, the Egyptians probably saw themselves differently from other Africans. Therefore, the credit for building the civilization of Egypt belongs to black Africans. So, as one looks at the evidence, it is clear that the idea that ancient Egyptians were European or Asian is equally as absurd as saying that the ancient Greeks or Romans were black Africans.

The Kingdom of Kush

As Egypt was declining, a new kingdom was rising to the south in the land of Kush. We mentioned the kingdom of Kush in our study of Egypt, but the golden age of Kush would not until come after the decline of Egypt.

Like the Egyptians, the Kushites lived off of the Nile River, and their culture was very similar to that of the Egyptians. Before 1070 BC, the land of Kush was frequently invaded by the Egyptians seeking to capture the plentiful gold mines in the territory but who never held a strong grip in Kush. After Egyptian power subsided, the Kushites had time to grow in strength. The Kushite capital was Napata. It was once an Egyptian religious center and was sacred to the Egyptian god Amen. Most historians believe the Kushites also shared the Egyptians' same religion. The Libyans had ruled Egypt since 945 BC; however by 727 BC their control in Egypt was eroding, and the Kushites under King Piye invaded Egypt. King Piye was also a great builder. He was credited for rebuilding the temple of Amen in Gebel Barkal. Another interesting aspect about King Piye was that he was the first of the Kushite kings to be buried in a pyramid. The Kushites eventually built more pyramids than the Egyptians.

In time, King Piye's control in Egypt weakened, leaving his

successor Shabaka to reconquer Egypt. King Shabaka's invasion of Egypt marked the beginning of what many historians call the twenty-fifth dynasty. King Shabaka transformed the kingdom of Kush into a large empire that stretched from their land in modern day Ethiopia in the south to the cities of Tyre and Jerusalem in modern day Palestine. The capital of the empire, the city of Waset, became a great trade center and acquired wealth from all over the ancient world.

Simultaneously a new threat was rising in the east—the Assyrian Empire. The mighty Assyrians had already conquered most of the Middle East to the west of Mesopotamia. The only barrier between Kushite-controlled Egypt was the Land of Canaan. However, a very interesting event occurred that halted the Assyrian advance. An Assyrian army led by King Sennacherib of Assyria attempted to invade the kingdom of Judah. However, the Assyrian army was mysteriously destroyed overnight and was forced to retreat with as many as 187,000 casualties. There are many opinions about how the Assyrian army was destroyed. Many historians say it was a plague; however, in the Bible there is an account about the Assyrians invading Judah, and according to the Bible, the Israelites (the people of Judah) prayed to the Lord God, and he sent his angels to destroy the Assyrians. Of course, most people who do not believe in the Bible will be more inclined to believe the plague theory, but I still find it very interesting how accurately the Bible depicts the event.

The outcome of the destruction of the Assyrian army meant that the Kushites were on their way to world conquest. In 690 BC King Taharqa ascended to the throne. During the reign of King Taharqa, the Kushites conquered vast territory in North Africa, and some historians believe that the Kushites even conquered land as far as Gibraltar in modern day Spain. Taharqa's reign was the golden age of the empire, and he was probably the greatest of the Kushite kings. Taharqa also was a great builder; some historians believe he was almost as great as Rameses II. This was no doubt the height of not only the empire of Kush but also of black African world powers.

However, their power was short-lived. In 671 BC the Assyrians returned, and this time they seized northern Egypt from the Kushites. Although Taharqa was able to retake northern Egypt in 669 BC, the Assyrians returned and conquered all of Egypt. When King Tanwetamani ascended to the throne, he once again recaptured the city of Memphis in northern Egypt. Unfortunately, the Assyrians returned in 663 BC, but this time they pushed all the way to the Kushite capital of Waset. The Assyrians destroyed Waset and firmly established their control in Egypt. This marked the end of the Kushite Empire but not the end of the kingdom.

The kingdom of Kush occupied the lands south of Assyrian Egypt. Egypt was conquered again and again, constantly switching hands as new conquerors invaded. After the Assyrians were defeated, The Babylonian Empire gained control of Egypt, followed by the Persians, who attempted to invade Kush as well. However, the invasion of Kush was a disaster. The kingdom of Kush once again flourished through trade and the many gold mines in the area. As a result, Kush continued to fend off invasion from the foreign conquerors in Egypt who were eager to acquire the gold mines in Kush. The Kushites also continued to aid the Egyptians in revolts against the Greeks and the Romans. After a war with the Roman army that ended in a stalemate, Kush remained an independent state while many other nations fell to the Roman Empire. Kush began its eventual decline around 200 AD. Kush eventually became part of the kingdom of Axum, which marked the end of the kingdom of Kush.

The kingdom of Kush is remembered as one of the great early civilizations of the ancient world. When Rome was little more than a small city, Kush was a mighty empire. While the ancient Greeks were in a dark age of warring city-states, Kush was a unified nation and a prosperous trading center. Kush had a rich culture and a twenty-three-letter alphabet, which defies the idea that Africans had no written languages. Unfortunately today most school history textbooks don't even mention the kingdom of Kush, and the ones that do simply portray Kush as just a small, insignificant state. But hopefully with the new discoveries about African history, the textbooks will be rewritten.

Carthage

The next great African civilization we will look at is the mighty nation of Carthage located in modern day Tunisia off the North African coast. The origin of the Carthaginians is controversial. For a long time, people thought of Carthaginians as being a European or "white" civilization. However, in recent years historians and archaeologists have discovered that Carthaginians were of a very different origin. First of all, let's look at the facts about the founding of Carthage.

The city of Carthage was founded by the Phoenicians of the ancient city of Tyre. The Phoenicians were of Middle Eastern origin. From the city of Tyre, the Phoenicians sailed all over the world. They were sea merchants who sailed to the farthest parts of Europe all the way to the southern tip of Africa and even to distant lands such as India (mind you, this was before the Suez Canal). The Phoenicians also founded colonies in North Africa, Spain, and elsewhere in the Mediterranean, one of which was Carthage. The Phoenicians were of Middle Eastern origin. However, when they founded Carthage, there were already indigenous peoples living there of African descent. Many historians believe that the Phoenicians and the indigenous North Africans intermarried; thus, the Carthaginians were of African and Middle Eastern decent.

Historians generally agree that Carthage was founded in 814 BC. Carthage started out modestly being just one of many Phoenician trade posts. However, Carthage began to increase in wealth and power through trade and commerce. The city of Carthage was one of the most spectacular cities on earth at the time. The city's thick walls were (according to Roman accounts) around twenty miles long. Inside the city were barracks and stables that could house thousands of cavalry and tens of thousands of infantry. They also had stalls that housed around three hundred war elephants. The city had two harbors, one for their over two hundred warships and the other for merchant vessels. On a more societal note, the city of Carthage was very advanced. The city was filled with libraries, theaters, and even public restaurants. The houses had pipes and drainage systems. It is also believed that they had a garage collection system similar to what we have today (almost three thousand years ago).

The Carthaginians, like the Phoenicians, were great seafarers and went on many explorations. They made explorations and established colonies as far as Britain in the north and all the way to West Africa to the south. Some historians even think that the Carthaginians may have visited the Americas.

Carthage by 300 BC had control over many, if not most, of the maritime trade routes during its time. Merchant ships from all over the world passed through Carthage, importing resources like gold, iron, silver, and many goods. Of course, in order to maintain their control of the trade routes, they had to have a functional army and powerful navy. The Carthaginian army was made up of mercenaries from Africa and the Mediterranean. The Carthaginians also had a formidable cavalry. But probably one of the most famous images of the Carthaginian army was its war elephants, who could wreak havoc on their enemies. The Carthaginian navy, unlike their army, was made up of native Carthages, many of whom were experienced seamen. Their navy had as many as three hundred ships, plus their tactical strategies, which gave them a strong advantage in sea battles. At the time, the Carthaginian navy was one of the largest and most experienced in the entire world.

As Carthage grew in power, it began to conquer other African nations in the south. The Carthaginian Empire acquired plenty of wealth in these new territories. This, however, made the surrounding nations very bitter against Carthage, making them eager to ally with foreign enemies of Carthage, such as the newly rising nation of Rome.

Conflict between the Carthaginians and the Romans erupted in 264 BC with a dispute between Carthage and the city of Messina on the island of Sicily. Originally, Messina had appealed to both Rome and Carthage for help in war against a rival city on the island. The city of Messina then suddenly changed allies and asked the Romans for help against a garrison of Carthaginian troops, which were originally sent to aid Messina. According to some sources, the people of Messina feared that Carthage would seize control of all of Sicily after war between the rival cities ceased. But whatever caused the change in alliances, Carthage became at war with Rome.

The Carthaginian navy was of course stronger and more experienced at naval warfare than the small Roman navy. So, in the beginning, the war went very well for Carthage. The war on land also went very well. Following a successful naval victory against the Romans, a Carthaginian army, led by a mercenary named Xanthippus, engaged in battle with a Roman army that had landed in North Africa, and the Battle of Bagradas ensued. The outcome was a decisive victory. As the dust lifted from the battlefield, Carthage seemed unstoppable.

However, the Roman navy developed new naval tactics that soon evened the odds of the war. This new tactic was the use of a device called the *corvus*, which was like a bridge that could be attached to the deck of a Carthaginian ship. With this device, the famous Roman legions could board the ships and basically turn a naval battle into a land battle. With the use of this corvus device, the Romans then had the advantage and dealt many serious defeats to the Carthaginian navy. The war continued to rage on, and many casualties were suffered on both sides, but in 241 BC, the Romans dealt the final blow that forced the

Carthaginians to negotiate peace with Rome. However, the Roman demands were severe and hostile.

The treaty between Carthage and Rome lasted a little more than twenty years; in 219 BC, a Carthaginian general by the name of Hannibal invaded the city Saguntum in modern day Spain. Saguntum was an ally of Rome, and when the Roman senate learned of the attack, it declared war against Carthage. Carthage responded by sending Hannibal to attack Rome. To reach Rome, Hannibal's army had to cross the Alpine mountain range. It was during the winter, and some of his troops perished in the bitter cold weather. However, Hannibal's army was still strong enough to do battle with the Romans and marched south into Italy. He reached northern Europe in the summer. Like Carthage, Rome had imposed its imperial rule over the local peoples; thus, these peoples (mainly Gauls and Celts) were quick to ally themselves with Hannibal. In the Battle of the Trebia River, Hannibal brilliantly ambushed a Roman army, killing as many as thirty thousand Roman soldiers. The Roman senate responded by sending another Roman army, under General Varro, to destroy the Carthaginians at the plains of Cannae in 216 BC. Varro's army numbered as many as eighty thousand foot soldiers, plus an additional seven thousand cavalry. Despite the Romans' numerical advantage, Hannibal engaged the Roman army in what became known as the Battle of Cannae.

The Battle of Cannae has gone down in history as one of greatest battles. It was a classic battle where an outnumbered army defeated an army more than twice its size. The Roman general Varro was utterly outmaneuvered and destroyed. When the armies met, the Roman general planned to use his numerical advantage by simply marching his force straight into to the Carthaginians to overwhelm them. He wisely deployed his cavalry on both sides of his infantry to protect his army from being attacked from the rear. The Roman cavalry, however, were not as experienced as Hannibal's mercenary cavalry. Hannibal's infantry marched in a bow-shaped formation with the belly of the bow facing the enemy. His more experienced cavalry were deployed on both sides of his main force.

Just before the main armies clashed, Hannibal's cavalry quickly attacked the Roman cavalry on both sides; soon afterward, the infantries also clashed, and a bloody battle ensued. Without much trouble, the Carthaginian cavalry routed the Roman horsemen. During that same time, Hannibal ordered his infantry in the center of the formation to slowly give ground; all the while the infantry on the sides held their position. This changed the army's bow formation into a concave formation. As the center began to collapse, the Romans perceived that victory was near and advanced straight into the center of the Carthaginian concave formation. Soon Hannibal's concave formation developed into a U-shape, with the Roman army in the middle. On

Hannibal's order, the U-shaped formation began closing in, attacking the Roman legions from three sides. With the Roman cavalry destroyed, the Carthaginian cavalry then attacked the Romans from behind, cutting off all escape. With the Roman army completely encircled, its numerical advantage was lost. They were then packed tightly together and could hardly maneuver. By the end of the battle, over sixty-five thousand Roman soldiers were killed, yet the Carthaginians lost only fifty-five hundred soldiers and two hundred cavalry. Hannibal was no doubt one of the greatest generals in history; never had the Roman legions suffered such losses in one day as they did on the plains of Cannae.

However, another Roman army, under General Scipio, counterattacked by invading Spain, seizing Carthage's gold and silver mines. In 206 BC the nation of Namibia declared war with Carthage and urged for Scipio to help them fight Carthage in North Africa. With the war on the African mainland, Hannibal was called back to Carthage to fight the Romans and their allies. Hannibal met the Romans and Namibians at the Battle of Zama. With the help of the Namibian horsemen, Rome and its allies defeated Hannibal at Zama in 202 BC. The defeat at Zama ended the war, and Carthage was forced to give up much of its territory in Africa and was also forced to reduce its navy to only ten ships. It also had to pay a harsh amount of tribute to Rome for the next fifty years.

Carthage recovered very well after the war. Once again the land flourished and prospered and trade and commerce were revived. The Carthaginians were so prosperous that they even proposed to pay the entire amount of tribute in just ten years. This made the Romans uneasy, and they refused. The Romans also went as far as having Hannibal exiled. In 151 BC, Carthage had paid all of the demanded tribute and continued to prosper. The Romans then decided to destroy the city of Carthage, but before they declared war with Carthage, the Romans demanded that Carthage surrender all its weapons so that hostilities would subside. Unfortunately, Carthage was deceived and agreed. After the weapons were secured, Rome declared war on Carthage and ordered the people of Carthage to leave the city so it could be destroyed. The people of Carthage then realized that war was inevitable, but they no longer had any weapons to resist the Romans. However, the Carthaginians resolved to fight with whatever they had.

In 149 BC the Roman army marched against Carthage, whose people were determined to die before they let their glorious city be destroyed. It took the Roman army three years to breach the city's walls. It is remarkable how it took the Romans, armed with catapults and other siege weapons, three years to subdue a determined people armed with anything they could find. By 146 BC, however, the Roman army stormed the city and slaughtered over two hundred fifty thousand people and sold fifty thousand into slavery. The city of Carthage was burned, and some theories suggest that the Romans sowed salt on the land so that it could not be farmed. The many libraries of Carthage were also burned to the ground, including those with five hundred thousand volumes of Carthaginian literature. The year 146 BC marked the end of the nation of Carthage.

However, the legacy of the nation of Carthage did survive the flames. The city of Carthage itself was one of the most advanced cities of its time. It was also the home of one of the world's greatest generals, Hannibal, whose armies routed the legendry Roman legions. Even when all hope for victory was lost, the people of Carthage fought until the very end. Carthage will forever have its place in ancient African history.

The Moorish Empire

With the destruction of Carthage, North Africa was mostly ruled by foreign conquerors, and after the conquest of Greco-Egypt, North Africa was under the control of the Roman Empire. But as the Roman Empire began to collapse, waves of other foreign invaders gained temporary control of North Africa. The most notable of these were the Arabs, who make up the majority of the modern North African population. When the Arabs invaded North Africa in 698 AD, many of the native peoples fled south across the Sahara Desert. However, some stayed and were converted to Islam (the religion of the Arab invaders). These black Africans were called Moors. Like most of the great peoples in North Africa, people in the West have seemed to think the Moors were of European or Arabic origin, but, once again, when we look at the facts and not popular opinion, we begin to see a more accurate position. The Romans were the first people to call North Africa's black inhabitants "Moors" or "Maures." This tradition was continued throughout the ages. Even in some of Shakespeare's plays, the term "Moor" is used to depict a person in the play that had dark skin. One example of this is in Shakespeare's play *Othello*. And if you look at old European texts written during this time, the word "Moor" was the common term used to describe people whose skin was black or brown. So the Moors, despite popular opinion, were of black African origin and were the founders of yet another great African civilization.

With all of North Africa under Islamic control, an Arab by the name of Musa ibn Nusair was appointed governor of North Africa. Nusair, however, was interested in invading Spain, which was ruled by King Roderick of the Visigoths. But the Visigoth defenses were formidable, so Nusair would put aside his ideas of conquest for the time being. However, in 711 AD, his chance came. There was a disagreement between King Roderick and the captain of the fortress that defended Spain's southern coast. This treacherous captain gave Nusair information about King Roderick's coastal defenses. With knowledge of the Visigoth defenses, Nusair sent an invasion force of about seven thousand Moor soldiers under Tariq ibn Ziyad to take Spain. Tariq's forces conquered city after city, and as they advanced northward, many native Spaniards joined him in hopes of overthrowing the oppressive Visigoths. King Roderick and his army, numbering about sixty thousand, met Tariq and his allies, numbering only about fourteen thousand. The two armies met at Janda Lagoon near the coast. The outcome of the battle was a noteworthy victory for Tariq, who continued his campaign until he was defeated by the Franks (medieval term for French) led by Charles Martel at the Battle of Tours in 732 AD.

There are many different opinions on the importance of the Battle of Tours. For years many Christians in the West have believed that the Battle of Tours was a last stand for Christianity worldwide. But this is not true. As many historians make new discoveries about African history, they find that there were (and are) black African Christians who lived south of the Sahara Desert. Now at first this may surprise some of you, but did not Jesus commanded his disciples to preach the Gospel all over the world? And there were many Africans in the Roman Empire during Jesus's time who were responsible for bringing the Gospel to their people back in Africa. Even whole nations accepted the Gospel. One of these nations was the kingdom of Axum in the land of Kush (modern day Ethiopia). However, after the Arab invasion, most of the African Christians in North Africa retreated to lands south of the Sahara Desert, and we will study these nations in the next chapter. Consequently, the Battle of Tours simply saved Christianity in Europe, more specifically in France. The Moors, however, still controlled almost all of Spain, and it is in Spain that Moorish culture flourished.

With the invasion of the Iberian Peninsula complete, the Moors settled in Spain, and Moorish culture had a lasting impact on Spanish culture. The Moors were responsible for much of the technology and societal progress that Spain experienced during the Middle Ages. Some historians even credit Moorish Spain for bringing modern civilization to Western Europe. Now how could this be? After the fall of the Roman Empire, Europe descended into the Dark Ages. Many Western historians have thought that during the

Middle Ages the entire world declined into a "dark age." However, this is one of the most infamous misconceptions of our time. While Europe was in an age of violence and instability, much of the rest of the world was advancing in civilization—civilizations like the ancient Mayans, Aztecs, and Inca in Central and South America; the Chinese, Arab, and Indian civilizations in Asia; and the ancient Ghanaian, Axumite, and Malian civilizations in Africa. So this "dark age" idea really only pertains to Europe (with the exception of Moorish Spain). Thanks to the Moors, Spain, unlike the rest of Europe at that time, had schools, colleges, and even universities. But it does not stop there.

The Moorish city of Cordova was one of the greatest cities in Europe, let alone the world. According to a census taken in 978 AD, Cordova had over two hundred thousand houses, many of which even had indoor plumbing. Cordova also had as many as sixty thousand palaces and mansions, around eighty thousand stores, and many libraries. One of these libraries had over four hundred thousand books on subjects ranging from mathematics and science to medicine and philosophy. Moorish Spain was also responsible for producing several tens of thousands of handwritten books each year. This market was in response to the growing demand for knowledge around the world. Most importantly, many of these schools and libraries were open to the public. Moorish Spain was also known for its religious tolerance of Moslems, Jews, and Christians, who all lived together in peace.

However, in later years, the Moorish caliphs (a Muslim governor or ruler) began to decline in power, and Moorish Spain soon fell into severe political unrest. This unrest eventually led to the collapse of the Umayyad Dynasty in 1031 AD. Yet, the history of Islamic Spain does not end there.

In 1052 AD a new Muslim power was rising: the Berbers. The Berbers were descendants of the Numidians (whose cavalry helped the Romans defeat the Carthaginians during the Punic Wars). Starting around 1048 AD, the Arab Muslims attempted to convert the Berbers to Islam. However, very few attempts were successful. Berbers who did convert to Islam were known as Almoravides. By 1052 AD, the Almoravides numbered as many as thirty thousand strong, and under their general Yahya, the Almoravides invaded Morocco. With the conquest of Morocco, the Almoravides established the Almoravid Empire in 1062 AD with the city of Marrakech as its capital.

It was during this time that Moorish Spain was under attack by Spaniards. As the pressure grew, the Moorish governor of the city of Seville implored to the newly founded Almoravid Empire for assistance against the onslaught. Yusuf ibn Tashfin (the Almoravid emperor at the time) responded quickly and raised a sizable army to come to the Moors' aid. Yusuf's forces battled the Spaniards at Zakah in 1086 AD and were victorious. After the Battle of

Zakah, Yusuf was made emperor of all Moorish Spain, and the Almoravid Empire became the "Empire of Two Shores." It is also important to mention that Yusuf and his army were of African descent, not Arab. For instance, the Catalan Atlas, which is a famous old Spanish map, depicts Yusuf as a black African.

Also during Yusuf's rein, the Moors constructed several forts in many different Spanish cities to defend against Spaniard attacks (and many of these forts still stand in Spain today). But one of the most important aspects of Yusuf's rein was that he preserved Moorish culture in Spain. With the influence of Moorish culture, Spain continued to be the most advanced nation in all of Europe.

However, there was a growing problem. When the Moors invaded Spain back in 711 AD, they did not completely destroy the Visigoths and Spaniards. These survivors established several small kingdoms in northern Spain and slowly began to regain strength. Starting around 900 AD, these kingdoms began to retake parts of Spain. These efforts soon became known as the Reconquista, and gradually more and more of Spain was seized from the Moors. The fall of Moorish Spain became more evident when the glorious city of Cordova was captured by the Spaniards in 1236. And by 1300 AD most of Spain was under Spanish control. Moorish Spain was paying tribute to placate the inevitable Spanish invasion. This invasion began after the marriage of King Ferdinand and Queen Isabella, which united the kingdoms of Aragon and Castille (two of the most powerful Spanish kingdoms). Together Ferdinand and Isabella waged war against the Moors and in 1491 besieged Granada, the new Moorish capital. Within a year, Granada fell to the Spaniards, which marked the end of Moorish Spain.

After the fall of the Roman Empire in 480 AD, Europe plunged into an age of darkness. This age of darkness lasted for the next thousand years. Basically all of Europe had sunk into barbarism, except Moorish Spain. When the rest of Europe was consumed in the wars and crusades, the Moors studied science and mathematics. The Moors were also responsible for reintroducing universities and the idea of public education to Europe. As I said earlier, it is arguable to say that it was the influence of Moorish culture on Europe that triggered the beginning of modern Western culture.

After the Spaniards retook Spain, they banished almost the entire Moorish population. Any remaining Moors or Muslims were forced to accept Catholicism. As a result, Spain declined sharply in civilization. Spain was no longer known for its great scientists and mathematicians or its elaborate libraries and palaces. In a way Spain seemed to also slip back into a Dark Ages civilization. However, Moorish culture forever left its mark on Spanish culture and civilization. Just go and visit modern Spain and you will find old Moorish buildings and even Moorish forts constructed by Yusuf almost one thousand years ago.

After the end of Moorish Spain, North Africa was ruled by Arabs from the Middle East. This is why Islam is the dominate religion in North Africa today. This is also why today many people believe that the Egyptians and Carthaginians had light complexions. However, if people go back and study the history of Africa, they learn that before the Arab invasion of North Africa during the late seventh century, Africa was inhabited by dark-skinned peoples. Of course, many people are still stubborn and will believe what they want to believe, but the facts and the evidence stand the test of time.

The Arabs continued to occupy North Africa for centuries until European nations like Britain and France invaded and controlled North Africa for more than a century. At the dawn of the twentieth century, the European domination of North Africa seemed impregnable. However, during World War II, when many of these European world powers engaged in a bloody war that devastated and severely weakened the nations of Europe, the Arabs, of course, seized this chance to regain their independence from the much-reduced European world powers. Despite this disadvantage, many of the European powers would not simply surrender North Africa to the Arab inhabitants, so the Arabs fought many bloody wars before they finally freed themselves of European rule. But by 1970 North Africa was again ruled by the Arabs and has remained so ever since.

This concludes our study of North Africa. For those of you who are interested in studying more about the history of North Africa, look up and read the many books that I have listed in the bibliography section of this book. Now that we have completed our brief study of North Africa, we will move on and learn about the many all-but-forgotten nations and civilizations of East Africa.

(Church in Lalibela, Ethiopia)

Chapter 2: East Africa

The history of East Africa began when Kush, one of the four sons of Ham, settled in the land of Kush (modern day Ethiopia) around 2800 AD. From there the sons of Kush dispersed and in time became the founders of many wealthy and powerful nations. Unfortunately today when studying world history, very few books even mention these nations. Many history books say that, for the most part, East African history did not really start until the arrival of the Europeans in the sixteenth century. But really this is based on the old prejudiced assumption that before the arrival of Europeans, Africa was nothing but a mysterious, backward continent. Some of these texts use the term "the

Dark Continent" to convey the image of jungles filled with half-naked, warlike tribes. But in modern times, archaeologists have uncovered the remnants of great civilizations and even empires that thrived in this region. Many of these nations engaged in trade with other well-known civilizations in the Middle East, India, and even China. With that in mind, let's dive into the truly rich history of East Africa before the arrival of the Europeans.

Ethiopia

One of the first great nations that flourished in East Africa was Ethiopia. The Ethiopians (Kushites) have lived in Ethiopia for over three thousand years. The first history book to mention the Ethiopians was the Bible. According to the Bible, the Ethiopians marched with the Egyptians against the kingdom of Judea back around 900 BC. The Bible states in 2 Chronicles 14:9 that the Ethiopians once fielded an army numbering one million men. Note that this was almost thousand years ago. No other army in the Bible is recorded to have had an army that numerous at that time, so obviously the Ethiopians were much more than just a small, insignificant tribe. The Bible also mentions in 2 Chronicles chapter nine that during the reign of King Solomon, the Queen of Sheba came to meet King Solomon in person and later lavished him with many gifts, such as gold and ivory. The Queen of Sheba is believed to have ruled in the land of Ethiopia. The Kushites later went on to conquer the decaying Egyptian Empire and spread their culture and influence all the away to the Iberian Peninsula in modern day Spain. However, because most of the Kushite Empire was based in Egypt, we studied about that period in the last chapter. After the Assyrian invasion of Kushite-occupied Egypt in 663 BC, the Kushites declined back to a kingdom in Ethiopia. During this time, the Kushites fought many foreign invaders, like the Persians and the Greeks as well as the Romans, who were all seeking to acquire the valuable gold mines and other resources in the region. By 200 AD, the Kushite Kingdom slowly began to decline, which gave rise to the next great Ethiopian kingdom.

The next great civilization to rise out of Ethiopia was the kingdom of Axum. The kingdom of Axum was not only one of greatest nations in the history of East Africa, but it was also one of the greatest Christian kingdoms in Africa. Axum is located in the modern day country of Ethiopia. For some of you, it may be hard to believe that there were Christian nations in Africa. However, if you remember, Jesus instructed his disciples to preach the Gospel to all peoples and nations, and when you look at a world map, Africa and Ethiopia are geographically just as close if not closer to Israel than Europe. For example, the Ethiopian Orthodox Church, which still exists today, traces its founding back to around 330 AD. This was also around the same time that the Catholic Church was founded by the Roman emperor Constantine. So, when you examine these important facts, it is quite clear that Christianity, in fact, took root in Africa as well as in Europe.

But now how exactly did Christianity take root in Ethiopia? The story of the conversion of Ethiopia was recorded by a church historian named Rufinus. According to Rufinus, a Middle Eastern philosopher by the name of Meropus set out on a voyage destined for India. He was accompanied by two young boys, Frumentius and Aedesius. However, on their way to India, they ran short of supplies and attempted to dock at a nearby port off the coast of Ethiopia. Apparently the people at this port were hostile to anybody associated with the Romans, and Meropus's ship was a Greco-Roman craft. When they reached the port, the inhabitants proceeded to slay all aboard the ship, yet Frumentius and Aedesius were spared the sword.

The two boys were later taken to the Axumite court and brought before King Ella Amide of Axum. The boys found favor with the king, and Frumentius was appointed as his royal treasurer and his secretary. Aedesius was made the king's cupbearer. As the king's treasurer and secretary, Frumentius rose to great prominence in Axum. When King Ella died, Frumentius was invited to assist the queen in governing the nation until the king's son was of age to rule. With this new position in government, Frumentius encouraged the spread of Christianity all over Axum and Ethiopia. Soon, Christianity spread and permeated the entire county. When the king's son was of age to rule, Frumentius became the first bishop of the Ethiopian Church. The king's son, King Ezana, also accepted Christianity and made it the national religion. Before this great revival, most Axumites worshipped the false deity Mahram. According to historians, Mahram bore the image of a serpent and was of ancient Persian origin. Early Axumite coins were minted with the image of Mahram. However, after Axum's conversion to Christianity, later coins were minted with the sign of the cross in reverence to Christ. These coins were also the first in the world to bear a Christian design.

Axum continued to excel in prominence and wealth and was one of the most influential nations the in the area after Rome and Persia. During this time the Axumite king built elaborate cathedrals carved out of solid rock, like Saint Mary of Zion, which is one of the oldest cathedrals on earth. The Axumites also engaged in trade with nations and provinces like Rome, Persia, and even China. They are also credited to have written great works of literature using their own written language. Some historians even rank Axum as one of the world's greatest nations at that time.

However, around the sixth century AD, Emperor Kaleb of Axum sent an Axumite army numbering seventy thousand men to assist Christians in Yemen (southern Arabia) who were engaged in a civil war with local Jews. The Axumites were victorious, but the Axumite general, General Abraha, for some reason suddenly proclaimed himself emperor of Yemen. He won many converts, but his religious zeal led him to attack the pre-Islamic city of Mecca. The city of Mecca, prior to Mohammed and the rise of Islam, was an important religious city to the Arab people. As a result of the attack on Mecca, the people of Arabia implored to the king of Persia for aid. The Persian army defeated the Axumites in Yemen in 572 AD, and Yemen was made a Persian territory.

After the defeat at Yemen, Axumite power was confined to Ethiopia, where it continued to prosper. But this all changed during the rise of Islam. After the Muslims conquered the Middle East, they began to invade North Africa. The North Africans either fled south into Sub-Saharan Africa or converted to Islam. Axum, however, with its strong Christian roots, remained a Christian kingdom but not without persecution. By the seventh century AD, Axum was encompassed by Islamic kingdoms on all sides, and war was inevitable. Axum's key seaport in the Red Sea, Adule, was attacked and destroyed by the Islamic nomads. The destruction of Port Adule meant that Axum was cut off from trade in the Red Sea. This led to a sharp decline in wealth and regional hegemony. However, Axum would not convert to Islam. The surrounding Islamic nations launched endless attacks against Axum, but the Axumites remained strong. As the persecution of Christians increased in surrounding lands, many of these persecuted Christians fled to Ethiopia. Axum, encompassed by enemies, fought for its survival for the next one thousand years. In time Axum became one of the last Christian kingdoms in Africa, and for the next one thousand years, Axum was like a refuge for Christians persecuted in Africa.

Now, some people might begin to think that Christianity had become a detriment to Axum. After all, being cut off from trade and commerce with other nations, Axum was basically cut off from wealth itself, for back then and even now trade was and is one of the main ways of attaining wealth. The West African kingdom of Mali, for example, during the fourteenth century, became one of the richest nations on the earth at the time, and it acquired its wealth and power through the control of key trade routes. We will go over the history of Mali in the next chapter.

As for the Ethiopians, they sacrificed wealth and prestige to follow the Christian god. Several centuries later, during the dawn of the European conquest of Africa, the European armies, armed with guns and other firepower, began to conquer the nations of Africa. African nations like Songhay, the Asante, the Zulus, Conge, and even Arab-ruled Egypt all fell to European powers. In the process of this invasion, hundreds of thousands of Africans perished, and the many once-glorious African kingdoms were erased. By the year 1914, almost all of Africa was under European control—that is, with the exception of Ethiopia. Although many other African nations, such as the Zulu and the Asante, put up a powerful resistance, they were eventually defeated. Ethiopia, however, was the only African nation to actually remain independent of foreign rule during this time. It is quite interesting that Ethiopia was also one of the only African nations that remained Christian during the wave of Islamic influence in African in the medieval era. Some Christian historians believe that because Ethiopians were faithful to their God for over a thousand years, they were protected from the invasion of the European powers of the nineteenth century.

This theory is somewhat proven true when you look at the history of Ethiopia. It was one of the last Christian nations in Africa and the last independent African nation during the colonial period. Ethiopia did, or course, have to fight to remain independent. One of the most decisive battles the Ethiopians fought against the European forces was the Battle of Adowa.

In this particular battle, Italy sent an army numbering twenty-five thousand soldiers to embark on a campaign to conquer Ethiopia in 1896. The Ethiopian army numbered about one hundred thousand foot soldiers and horsemen, most of who were armed with guns. Now, at first, this might have appeared to be an obvious advantage for the Ethiopians. However, the Italian army possessed some of the latest weaponry of the century. Weapons such as machine guns, artillery, and repeating rifles could devastate any army in their way. Many African armies, for the most part, did not have artillery and other firepower at that time, and guns used by some African nations at the time were mostly outdated and had much shorter range and less accuracy compared to the guns used by the Europeans. So, despite their numerical advantage, the Ethiopian army, because of its lack of modern weaponry, was really at a disadvantage, for during this age of warfare, massive African armies were completely destroyed by relatively small European armies.

Armed with powerful rifles and artillery, the Italians were

confident of victory. However, on the day of the battle, the Italians made a detrimental mistake. The Italian general, after being given inaccurate information about the Ethiopians' position, ordered his forces to advance further in to the Adowa Valley. However, they ended up walking right into the Ethiopian forces, and the Ethiopians had both the high ground and the element of surprise. One interesting fact about this is that prior to the Italians' fateful move, the Ethiopians were engaged in what some historians called "a religious gathering for prayer." Yet, as we learned earlier, the Ethiopians were Christians, so this "religious gathering" was mostly a prayer to their God, Jesus, for favor in the upcoming battle. And surprisingly, it was during this prayer gathering that the Italians walked into a fatal trap that turned the tide of the battle. When the scouts reported the Italians' position, the Ethiopian generals ordered a counterattack.

With the Ethiopians firing a hail of bullets down on the approaching army, the Italians, despite their advantage of firepower, were unable to advance farther and began to retreat. However, the Ethiopian cavalry overtook the retreating Italians and slaughtered thousands of them. In the end, the Italian army in their hasty retreat left behind most of their guns and artillery. In all, the Ethiopians captured over twelve thousand high-quality guns and many pieces of artillery. At the end of the day, over seven thousand Italians were killed and several more thousand captured. Ethiopian casualties were about five thousand killed and over eight thousand wounded. But Ethiopia was free and remains independent to this today.

As a nation, Ethiopia is a symbol of independence for the rest of Africa. Although modern Ethiopia was founded in 1896, Ethiopian history began over three thousand years ago with the nation of Kush. The early Christian nation of Axum is remembered for its unyielding stand for Christ in the midst of Islamic nations on all sides. Axum is also noted for its magnificent churches and cathedrals carved out of solid rock. Some historians believe that two of these churches in particular should be wonders of the world. Today Ethiopia is one of the oldest nations in Africa and remains a symbol of freedom to the African world—a freedom that some believe it has maintained because the Ethiopians were faithful to Christ.

The Nubian Kingdoms

During the decline of Kush in the fourth century AD, new nations began to rise and eventually replaced Kush. The people of Nubia, who inhabited the Blue Nile valley south of Kush, were rapidly growing in power. In time the Nubians erected fortresses as large as those in Kush and Roman-occupied Egypt.

The Nubian peoples formed three individual kingdoms: Nobadia in the south, Makuria in the center, and Alwa to the south. These kingdoms bordered Roman-occupied Egypt, and as the Roman Empire began to weaken, the Nubian nation of Nobadia took an aggressive stance against Roman-occupied Egypt. At first the Romans tried to placate Nubian aggression with annual subsidies; however, the Nobadae continued their raids into Egypt. In 452 AD the Romans responded with force and successfully drove the Nobadae out of Egypt and ratified the peace treaty. This treaty lasted until the fall the Roman Empire less than fifty years later and after which the Nobadae proceeded to seize Egypt.

With the fall of the Roman Empire in the early sixth century, the three Nubian kingdoms became the world powers of the Nile valley. The capital of the Nobadae was Faras, and the Nobadae ruled from the first to the third cataract of the Nile. The kingdom of Makuria ruled the lands between the third and fourth cataracts and ruled from their capital at Old Dongola. The kingdom of Alwa ruled the regions between the fourth and fifth cataracts. Relations between the Nobadae and Alwa were mainly peaceful; however, the Nobadae were often at war with the Makurians.

For the most part, the Nubian kingdoms worshipped Isis, an ancient god of the Egyptians; however, the Nubian kingdoms converted to Christianity in 531 AD. Christianity spread all throughout Nubia, and the kingdoms of Nubia were radically changed. Old temples like the temple of Isis (an ancient god of the Egyptians) were used as church buildings for the many new converts. The early medieval kingdoms of Nubia are another example of Christianity in Africa at a very early date. However, some historians believe that Christianity reached Nubia earlier that 531 AD, and they base this theory on earlier writings that date around 450 AD. One of these writings is an inscription in the Temple of Mandulis about a Nubian king by the name of Silko. One part that stands out is where it states, "On two occasions I fought with the Blemmyes and *God* gave me the victory." The inscription does not identify who this "God" is, so we cannot just assume that King Silko was a Christian. Yet, in addition to old writings, there were old pieces of pottery that bore Christian symbols that were also dated during the fifth century AD, so the matter is still controversial. Maybe Christianity did reach Nubia earlier than 531AD, but it was not until the sixth century that Christianity took root there.

After their conversion, the Nubian kingdoms became allies with the Byzantine
Empire. (Toward the end of the fifth century, the Roman Empire split into the Western and Eastern Roman Empires. The Eastern Roman Empire [Byzantium], which was based mostly in Asia, remained several centuries after the fall of the Western Roman Empire in 476 AD). It appears that the Byzantines were looking for allies to side with them against the Persian Empire.

Like Kush before it, Nubia flourished and prospered. The Nubian kingdoms attained much wealth, not by war but by trade. It is believed that the Nubian kingdoms were ruled by monarchs with almost absolute power and authority. Yet, Nubia still seems to have prospered under this rulership. Under their powerful king, the Nubians built many great forts and palaces lavished with gold and imported materials, such as clothes, Persian rugs, silk, and even Chinese pottery. According to an Arab historian, Abu Salih, the Nubian kingdom of Alwa alone had over four hundred churches and cathedrals. The Nubian Church became a powerful institution in Nubia, although it still answered to the Byzantine Orthodox Church in Alexandria, Egypt.

However, in the seventh century, a new power began to rise

in Arabia: Islam. Up to this point the Arab peoples of the Arabian Peninsula were mostly either nomads or merchants. After the teachings of Mohammed, however, the Arab peoples united and formed a new powerful force. Driven by religious zeal, the Arabs embarked on a quest to conquer the world for their god, Allah. The Arab forces stormed Byzantine-ruled Egypt in 639 AD and from there pressed farther into North Africa. By the next century, all of North Africa fell to Arab control. The Arabs then launched an invasion of Nubia in 642 AD. With an army numbering around twenty thousand men, Arabian forces penetrated deep into Nubian lands. However, the Nubian army counterattacked and inflicted severe casualties on the Muslims. This halted the Arab invasion of Sub-Saharan Africa and forced the Muslims to sign a peace treaty, which calmed hostilities for the time being.

The Nubians, however, broke the treaty and resumed their raids against Egypt. The Arabs responded by launching a second invasion of Nubia. An Arab army of five thousand cavalry besieged the Makurian capital of Old Dongola. Arab catapults battered away at the besieged city, destroying important buildings, including churches. The Nubians did fight quite valiantly and inflicted many casualties on the invaders. Perhaps the most valiant Nubian soldiers were their archers. The Arabs soon called these archers names like "The Archer of the Eyes" for their deadly accuracy. On one occasion in particular, a force of Arabs charged a band of Nubian archers but were beaten back by the intense volleys of arrows. This disastrous defeat was witnessed by an Arab sheikh who reported:

"I never saw a people who were sharper in war than they. I heard one of them say to the Muslims 'Where do you want me to hit you with my arrows?' And in case the Muslim would disdainfully say, 'In such a spot,' the Nubian would never miss it."

It was these Nubian archers who forced the Arabs to a stalemate. Another peace treaty was signed and hostilities again subsided.

Slowly, however, the hostilities between Arabian Egypt and Nubia increased during the following centuries. This tension was usually caused by violations of the peace treaty. By the eighth century, the Arabs and Nubians engaged in minor skirmishes. In the beginning the Arabs launched several successful skirmishes and took several people captive. However, later in the century, the Nubians gained the advantage. Under King Cyriacus the Nubians invaded Egypt. Apparently the Arab-Egyptians were holding several Christian leaders captive. Yet, the Arab governor refused to comply with Cyriacus's demand for their release. As a result, Cyriacus responded by invading Egypt with an army of one hundred thousand horsemen. The Nubian army reached as far as the city of Cairo before the Egyptian governor released the prisoners. Following this victory Cyriacus returned to Nubia.

But raids and skirmishes continued, and soon tensions reached a climax. In 833 AD the Nubian emperor sent his nephew to meet with the caliph of Baghdad to negotiate Arab incursions in Nubian territory. Negotiations were successful, and the treaty was ratified. But this treaty was nothing but a short pause in a war that lasted for centuries. By 854 AD war was resumed, but after a few minor battles, another short-lived treaty was signed. Shortly after this treaty, Makurian Nubians fell into a civil war between the Makurian emperor and his nephew. Apparently the emperor's nephew had agreed on the treaty with the Egyptians without the emperor's consent. The Makurian emperor then appointed one of his own sons to wage war with both the Egyptians and his nephew. The Makurian emperor emerged victorious, both capturing his treacherous nephew and driving out his nephew's Egyptian allies.

In 956 AD the Makurian Nubians again launched another attack against the Egyptian town of Aswan near the frontier. This campaign went badly for the Nubians, who were put on the defensive as Arab forces counterattacked, driving deep into Nubian territory and burning many towns as they advanced. After plundering and taking captive many prisoners, the Arabs returned to Egypt. Wars continued throughout the eleventh, twelfth, and thirteenth centuries.

However, in the in the thirteenth century, Nubia faced many challenges. One challenge was that many Arab peoples were taking over the northern parts of the kingdom. They did this by first trading with the Nubian cities to the north, and then many of these traders settled and intermarried with the people there. The problem was that these Arab immigrants did not acknowledge the rule of the Nubian king. Moreover, these Arab people who owned land in Nubia planned to pass it down to their children who would then pass it down to their children, creating a large population of Arab people living in Nubia. These Arab immigrants were Muslim, and soon Islam was spread through northern Nubia, a land that was originally Christian.

At the same time, the tide had turned in the war between Nubia and Egypt. Arabs from both Arabia and Egypt relentlessly attacked the Nubian kingdom of Makuria, killing and capturing many people. In 1276 the Arab sultan of Cairo, Egypt, launched another full-fledged invasion of Makuria. With the help of some Nubian traitors, the Arabs defeated the Makurian emperor, David. During this invasion many churches were burned to the ground while hundreds of people were slaughtered or taken prisoner. Following this victory the Arabs appointed a new king of Makuria, Shekanda, who was a traitorous relative of Emperor David. Shekanda was really more like a servant of the Egyptian sultan, paying him a hefty annual tribute.

From this time forward, much of Nubia remained under Arab rule. After the Arab conquest of the Nubian kingdom of Makuria, the remaining kingdoms of Nubia began to decline. The kingdom of Alwa was the last to fall to the Arab invaders in 1523. After the invasion of the Christian Nubia, remaining Christians fled to the Ethiopian kingdom of Axum. The land of Nubia was inhabited by Arab nomads who reduced many of the once-great Nubian cities to utter ruin.

Soon, after a thousand years of power, the Nubian kingdoms passed into history. In modern times very little is known about the Nubian kingdoms; however, this is changing as historians and archeologists continue to rediscover medieval Nubian ruins and writings. So, in time, we may know much more about the Christian kingdoms of medieval Nubia.

The Swahili States

Between 700 and 1500 AD the Swahili Confederation, which was made up of as many as fifty cities off the coast of East Africa, flourished due to their control of trade in the India Sea. Unfortunately today few people know about the Swahili states. Many history books say that the trade in the Indian Ocean was between Arab sailors and small, undeveloped tribes on the East African coast. However, again, this popular Western opinion says that most of Africa was inhabited by uncivilized tribal peoples. When one looks at Africa today, though, there are hundreds of old ruins and remains of sophisticated civilizations all over the continent that date centuries before the European invasion in the eighteenth century. And today in the modern nations of Somalia, Kenya, and Tanzania, there are remnants of city-states that flourished centuries prior to the European invasion.

Another common misconception is that the Swahili states were established by Arab merchants or even Indian settlers. Some would even say that they were an Arab civilization. Their main basis to this claim is the Arab influence on Swahili culture and language today—influences such as the numerous Arabic letters in the Swahili language as well as the Arab architecture in many modern East Africa cities. However, what many of these historians miss is that most of the Arab influence on the Swahili language was during a later period in history in the eighteenth century. It was during that time that the Arabs invaded East Africa and actually ruled established Arab kingdoms on the coast with the original inhabitants as their subjects and slaves. It was the influence of these Arab kingdoms that made the changes in the Swahili language that we see today.

Some historians persist that Swahili architecture has many resemblances to Arab architecture. However, when you think of it, Indian and Persian cultures resemble Arab culture, but all of these cultures have distinct differences that originated in their native lands. So would we call the achievements of the Indian peoples or of the Turks Arab achievements? No, we would not. So there really is no reason to give credit to the Arabs for the achievements of the East Africans.

Soon the Swahili states created an empire that the Arabs called Zanj. As always, trade and commerce brought wealth and power to the ones who controlled it, so Zanj by the ninth century had a thriving trade of ivory with India and even China. Ivory was used to craft the handles for weapons like swords and daggers as well as to make chairs and even chess pieces.

It is also believe by some historians that the Zanj also made voyages to India, Persia, and even to China. The Zanj made these trade voyages on ships called *dua la mtepe*. Vessels without sails were simply call mtepe. Now, the ships that the Zanj used were not little canoes. For example in 1414 AD, the Swahili city of Malindi sent a giraffe to the Chinese as a gift. Now it would be impossible to fit a giraffe in a small canoe, not to mention sailing the animal across the Indian Ocean, so evidently the Zanj sailed in seaworthy vessels.

By the fourteenth century, trade and commerce in the Indian Ocean were at a scale equal to that of the ancient Romans. The Zanj gained wealth and prominence all throughout the Oriental world, not by war and conquest but through commerce. Now, of course, every nation had an army. According to an Arab historian by the name of Al Masudi, who visited the Zanj in 916 AD, the Zanj emperor, known as Waqlimi, could rally an army of about three hundred thousand cavalry mounted on cattle instead of horses or camels. Compared to armies in Europe at that time, the Zanj army was massive. For example, when William the Conqueror invaded Britain in 1066, his army numbered only around twenty thousand to thirty thousand men.

The Zanj were also credited for smelting high-quality steel. Steel was of course used to craft weapons as well as tools. A weapon's quality was dependent on the quality of steel used to craft it. As a result, the Zanzibari iron trade prospered, and soon iron was the main export for many

Zanj cities. According to some historians, the quality of steel smelted by the Zanj was not surpassed until the nineteenth century.

After the end of the Shirazi Dynasty in the fourteenth century, the Zanj cities became the Swahili Confederation. Despite the breakup of the empire, each individual city continued to prosper. However, the Swahili Confederation came to a violent and abrupt end in the sixteenth century. The Portuguese, under Vasco da Gama, sailed to the coast and demanded the Swahili cities pay tribute to the king of Portugal and acknowledge his kingship. When the Swahili cities refused, the Portuguese unleashed a deadly assault and destroyed every city that defied them. After destroying all resistance, the Portuguese proceeded to plunder the burning cities, seizing large amounts of gold, silk, and anything else of any value.

One of the main reasons why the Portuguese were so successful in their conquest of the Swahili states was their use of guns and cannons. Now some historians might say that the fact that the Portuguese had firepower technology would imply that they were a more advanced civilization. This, however, is not necessarily accurate. If you read about European history in the sixteenth century, you notice that the living conditions for most of the common people were below average. In addition, things like personal hygiene were also dangerously low, which, of course, later led to disease. In fact, this lack of basic hygiene led to horrible plagues that spread throughout most of Europe. These plagues eventually led to the death of about a third of Europe's population. So even though the Europeans may have had superior firepower technology, socially Europe was still emerging from the Dark Ages. As a result, the Portuguese invasion did nothing to further civilization in East Africa.

After the fall of the Swahili states, most of the East African coast became a territory of the Portuguese Empire. Unlike later European invaders, the Portuguese did not colonize or redevelop the coast. They simply established trade sites and fortified their position with fortresses. However, they failed to make a substantial profit, and the once-prosperous African cities soon crumbled to ruin. The Portuguese ruled most of the East African coast for the next three hundred years until the Arab invasion in 1820. The Arabs then conquered the Portuguese and established their rule in the region. In many ways Arab rule was even more oppressive than Portuguese occupation. One example is the Arabs' enslavement of the coastal peoples. Arab slave raiders penetrated deep into Africa abducting thousands of Africans annually. This slave trade, of course, only inflamed hostilities already felt between the Arabs and Africans. Fortunately, the East African slave trade ended during the 1880s. However, shortly after the end of the East African slave trade, European nations, such as Britain and Germany, invaded.

The legacy of the Swahili states is unlike that of Egypt or Rome for the Swahili states attained their wealth from commerce and trade, not by war and conquest. Still there are some people who would like to credit the success and prosperity of the Swahili states to foreign peoples like the Arabs and Indians. Yes, Swahili culture may have resembled Arab culture, but does that make the civilization Arabic? In today's world, many modern nations from all different parts of the world all resemble each other but at the same time are all very different nations. For example, the modern nations of China and America both have similar architecture and other things along those lines. But ethnically America and China are very different, and we wouldn't call a modern building in China an American building. Neither would we call a modern building in America a Chinese building. In the same way, the Swahili nation, with all of its Arab culture and architecture, is still truly African, not Arab. As historian Basil Davidson states in his book *The Lost Cities of Africa*:

"These merchant cities and trading kingdoms of the coast of the Zanj, we may conclude, were neither Arabian nor Persian nor Indian: they were African, and predominantly negro African–just as were Timbuktu and Gao and Djenne, The kingdoms of the Hausa, the city-states of Ife and Benin."

After the fall of the Swahili states, Eastern Africa, much like North Africa before it, experienced an era of foreign rule. First came the Portuguese, who established forts along the coast. But the Portuguese were unable to master the art of trade like the Swahili before them, and soon the East African trade along the coast failed. With the exception of Ethiopia, this led to the eventual collapse of advanced African civilization along the coast.

(The Great Mosque of Djenné)

Chapter 3: West Africa

West African civilization reached its golden age mainly during the European Dark Ages. Some of first kingdoms of West Africa began to rise around the 300 AD. One of the important changes that sparked the rise of several mighty empires was the discovery and use of iron. This brought West Africa into the Iron Age and laid the foundation that gave rise to one of West Africa's great empires, Ghana. Just like the Hittites of Asia Minor in the Middle East, West African kingdoms that learned to use iron had a decisive advantage over their neighboring rival kingdoms. Armed with iron swords, lances, and iron arrowheads, these kingdoms conquered their neighbors and established powerful empires. Their kings were believed to be the rich men on earth during their time. But this wealth was attained not by tribute but by a monopoly in the Trans-Sahara trade routes.

The Trans-Sahara trade reached its height during the Middle Ages. Now, the Tran-Sahara trade routes were like the major highways between North Africa and Sub-Saharan Africa. North Africa was separated from the rest of Africa by the Sahara Desert, which is the largest desert on earth. As time progressed, Africans learned to use the camel as a means of transportation across the desert. As the Arabs of North Africa traveled through the desert to Sub-Saharan Africa, they came in contact with the peoples of Sub-Saharan Africa, and together they established trading centers. The Arab traders came for gold and ivory in exchange for salt, oil, and many other items from the Eastern world. The trade between North Africa and Sub-Saharan Africa flourished and brought great wealth to West Africa.

It is important to point out that although gold, salt, and ivory made up most of the trade in medieval Africa, slaves were also exchanged for goods. However, one should not equate this form of slavery with the Trans-Atlantic slave trade. Unlike the Trans-Atlantic slave trade, slaves in medieval Africa were typically debtors, prisoners of war, or criminals. Also in many pre-colonial African societies the children of slaves were born free. They were not held responsible for their parents' actions. In many African societies, slaves were generally seen as servants and were treated like human beings, not property. The Trans-Atlantic slave trade was completely different from pre-colonial African slavery.

The Empire of Ancient Ghana

The first major West African nation to rise to power in this region was Ancient Ghana in the modern day nation of Mali. The history of Ancient Ghana begins around the third century AD. One of the earliest cities of this region was Old Djenne, which is believed to have been founded around 250 BC, and by the sixth century AD, it had a population of over twenty thousand citizens. Medieval London, in comparison, only had a population of eight thousand at that time. Even from an early date, Old Djenne was the center of trade between North and Sub-Saharan Africa.

In the eighth century AD, Ghana began to expand and conquer rival kingdoms with their new weapon: iron. It was in the eighth century that the Ghanaians switched from using weapons made of copper or bronze to using iron swords and lances. Swords made of iron could often break weapons made of inferior metals. With the knowledge of iron, Ghana established dominion over most of its adversaries and forged its own empire. Soon the people of Ghana began to extensively mine for iron. This basically brought Ghana out of the Stone Age and into the Iron Age, which led them to a more sophisticated civilization. The Iron Age also enhanced agriculture by replacing wooded or stone farm tools with tools made of iron, which, of course, was more durable. This allowed Ghana to advance in other areas of civilization, such as commerce. As the Ghanaian Empire expanded, it soon controlled most of the Trans-Sahara trade routes.

Much of our knowledge about Ancient Ghana comes from the writings of medieval Arab explorers who documented their travels to distant lands. One of the first of these explorers to travel to Ancient Ghana was Ibn Fazari during the eighth century. Fazari described Ghana as the land of gold. A fourteenth century Arab historian, Ibn Khaldun, described the power of Ancient Ghana in his book *The Book of Roger* in which he stated:

"At the time of the conquest of northern Africa, some merchants penetrated into the western part of the land of the Blacks and found among them no king more powerful than the king of Ghana. His states extended westwards to the shores of the Atlantic Ocean. Ghana, the capital of this strong, populous nation was made up of two towns...and formed one of the greatest and best populated cities in the world".

Another Arab geographer by the name of Abu Ubayd Al-Bakri wrote a narrative on the Ancient Ghanaian capital city of Kumbi-Saleh. In his book, *The Book of the Roads and Kingdoms*, Al-Bakri stated that the people of Ghana wore cotton and even silk. But the wealth of Ghana did not come from conquest or tribute; Ghana's wealth was based in the Trans-Sahara gold and salt trade. Their capital city,

Kumbi-Saleh was a major center for trade with caravans for the north that brought salt and gold from the south. Ghanaian officials took advantage of this commerce and imposed import and export taxes (tariffs) that soon enriched the empire. Ghanaian merchants exchanged copper, leather, cloth, and iron goods. Arab geographer Ibn Haukal traveled to Ghana in the tenth century and saw with his own eyes the size of the Trans-Saharan trade routes. Haukal described the king of Ghana as the richest king on earth. One particular prosperous city of Ghana was Audoghast. Audoghast had merchants traveling all the way from Spain. Some historians argue that Ghana was the main source of gold for the Mediterranean world during the Middle Ages.

As gold flowed into Ghana, the kings of Ghana learned how to maintain the value of gold. According to the Arab historian Abu Ubaid:

"All nuggets of gold that are found in the mines of this empire belong to the king; but he leaves to his people the gold dust that everyone knows. Without this precaution gold would become so plentiful that it would practically lose its value."

In the ninth century, the Berber peoples from the Sahara in the north descended into West Africa and challenged Ghanaian sovereignty. After capturing many of the northern provinces and cities, they established their presence in Ghana. Under the leadership of Tilutane, the Berber army, numbering as many as ten thousand camel raiders, disrupted the Ghanaian trade routes. However, after the death of Tilutane the unity of the Berbers died with him. As the Berbers' power dwindled, the Ghanaians soon reconquered their lost territory.

Of course, with such an extensive empire, Ghana maintained a vast army. In the eleventh century, the Ghanaian army consisted of two hundred thousand foot soldiers as well as forty thousand cavalry. Now, to fully understand the great size of this army, you must understand that most armies of the time numbered an average of maybe forty thousand men. For example, in the Battle of Tours both armies numbered only eighty thousand strong each. William the Conqueror of Normandy's army that invaded England in 1066 only numbered fifteen thousand soldiers. So, an army numbering two hundred thousand men during that time was a testament to Ghana's power.

The first major threat to Ghanaian power after the Berbers was the rise of an African Islamic people by the name of the Almoravides. The Almoravides were determined to seize the city of Audoghast from Ghana. Due to the Berber invasion, Audoghast had a mainly Berber population; it was also the capital of the short-lived Berber Kingdom, which was formed under Tilutane. The Berbers, being new converts to Islam, resented being ruled by a non-Islamic nation. In

1055 AD the Almoravides seized control of Audoghast. In 1076, the Almoravides declared a holy war on all of Ghana. Driven by religious zeal, the Almoravides fought their way deep into Ghana in that same year, where they sacked the city of Kumbi-Saleh. It is important to point out that the Almoravides fought for more than a decade to subdue Ghana, which is interesting when considering that in Spain, the Almoravides defeated their enemies much more quickly. Their jurisdiction in Ghana was short-lived, however, for by 1087 the Almoravides had established their empire in Spain, and their hold on the territories in Ghana began to fade. The Ghanaians soon resumed control of their empire.

Ghana continued to be a prosperous kingdom, but Islam left an almost irremovable mark on Ghana as well as on West Africa. During the war with the Almoravides, Ghana was reduced almost to ruin. The Almoravide invaders devastated and plundered the land. During this period the authority of the Ghanaian king was all but destroyed. Ghana continued on, but, as time progressed, some parts of the empire rebelled and formed their own states to rival Ghana. One major rival was the city of Sosso, which raided Kumbi-Saleh. This led to civil war between the rival kingdoms. By 1240, the kingdom of Mali defeated Sosso and Kumbi-Saleh, as well as all other rivals, and soon became the new power in West Africa.

Medieval Ghana was the first of three great empires that

rose to great prominence from the eighth century all the way to the end of the sixteenth century. Ancient Ghana is also the kingdom that the modern day nation of Ghana named itself after. Also, it is interesting that Ghana is remembered not because of its armies, like many other empires were remembered, but because of its wealth, which it attained not through conquest but through commerce.

The Mali Empire

In the twelfth century, as Ghanaian power began to diminish, several cities gained their independence and established city kingdoms. The city kingdom of Sosso was often at war with Ghana and succeeded in raiding Kumbi-Saleh several times, and it appeared to soon be the next mighty kingdom in West Africa. However, Sosso soon took notice of another rising power, the kingdom of Mali. The kingdom of Mali had established itself as an independent kingdom in the early twelfth century, and conflict between these rival kingdoms soon led to war. The Sosso, led by King Sumanguru, devastated the Malian capital in 1224. The Sosso army burned the city and slew almost all of the royal family. One of the survivors was Prince Sundiata, whom Sumanguru spared because he was crippled. Several years later Sundiata overcame his disability and became the new ruler of Mali. Sundiata rallied the Malian army and led them in a guerrilla campaign against the kingdom of Sosso. Sundiata first led his army against weak rival kingdoms and recruited the conquered peoples into his army. In 1235 the Malian army marched against Sumanguru in the Battle of Kirina. The Malians emerged victorious and besieged and captured the Sosso capital. With the defeat of the Sosso, Sundiata soon conquered the Ghanaian capital. After this conquest, Sundiata returned to his capital city Djerba. In Djerba, Sundiata met with the rulers of the conquered kingdoms, who swore their loyalty to him in 1240, which marked the beginning of the Mali Empire.[4]

After the establishment of the empire, Sundiata shifted his focus from warfare to financial and societal development. Sundiata wisely permitted the rulers of the conquered kingdoms to retain their royal titles. Many former Malian soldiers soon became farmers. Lastly, Sundiata established a new capital city, Niani.

While Sundiata focused on developing the empire, his generals led further conquests. They conquered all the way up the coast of the Atlantic Ocean and all the land in between. This gave the Malians control of many important gold mines and also helped them establish new trade routes.

Sundiata was succeeded by Mansa Wali in 1255 ("Mansa" was the name for king or emperor). Mansa Wali's rule was quite peaceful and uneventful. His generals, however, conquered a couple of small kingdoms on the frontier. When Mansa Wali died in 1270, he left no heir, which led to a power dispute. Confusion followed and several men claimed the right to rule. The most successful of these men was Mansa Sakura who came to power in 1285. Under Sakura's rule, the empire flourished with merchants coming from territories as far as the Middle East. Also, gold flowed into the empire from the gold mines in the territory of Wangara. Some historians estimate that a total of 3,500 tons of gold was mined in West Africa before 1500.

Like Ghana, much of our knowledge about Mali comes from Arab travelers who traveled to these different empires during the Middle Ages (much the way European explorers like Marco Polo traveled to the Far East [China and India]). One of these travelers by the name of Ibn Fadl Al-Umari of Cairo, Egypt, wrote a book about his travels. In one chapter of his book he wrote an account about two great Mali voyages around 1300 AD. According to Ibn Fadl Al-Umari, a Malian emperor ordered a great maritime voyage to explore the extremity of the Atlantic Ocean. The fleet consisted of four hundred ships with two hundred packed with supplies to last two years at sea and two hundred filled with men. According to Umari only one ship returned. The emperor then decided to carry out the exploration himself. He assembled a truly massive fleet consisting of two thousand ships, half full of supplies and half filled with men. As far as Umari knew, they also did not return. Now, this raises an important question: did the Malians visit the Americas? According to some historians, archeologists unearthed two Negro skeletons in the Virgin Islands that dated around the thirteenth century. Other historians have discovered carvings that depict people wearing turbans and tattoos on their faces. Some historians believe that these carvings may have been depicting Malians because such art was popular in Mali during that time. If this theory is true, the Malians are credited for exploring the Americas

181 years before Columbus's exploration.

Back in West Africa, Emperor Mansa Musa came to the throne in 1312. Most historians regard him as being the greatest of the Malian emperors. Mansa Musa, being a Muslim, made a pilgrimage to the holy city of Mecca. He traveled with his royal caravan, which consisted of tens of thousands of men clothed in imported silk robes as well as eighty camels laden with three hundred pounds of gold each.

Along the way, the royal caravan stopped in Cairo, Egypt. According to some historians, Mansa Musa spent so much gold while visiting Egypt that the value of gold in Egypt plummeted and did not recover for several years. This pilgrimage captured world attention, and many people regarded the Malian Empire as a "mysterious land of gold." In many ways Mansa Musa's pilgrimage had an irremovable mark on world history.

Mansa Musa also brought stability to the empire. The famous medieval traveler Ibn Battuta, who visited the empire in the mid-fourteenth century, made this statement:

"The Negroes are seldom unjust, and have a greater abhorrence of injustice than any other people. Their sultan shows no mercy to anyone who is guilty of the least act of it. There is complete security in their country. Neither traveler

nor inhabitant in it has anything to fear from robbers or men of violence."

Mansa Musa was also a great builder. During his reign, he had several universities and mosques in his major cities like Gao and Timbuktu. There was a great hunger for knowledge in Timbuktu. Leo Africanus, who visited Timbuktu in the sixteenth century, said:

"In Timbuktu there are numerous judges, doctors and clerics, all receiving good salaries from the king. He pays great respect to men of learning. There is a big demand for books in manuscript, imported from Barbary. More profit is made from the book trade than from any other line of business."

It is important to point out that although the people of Timbuktu may have not had a written language in their native tongue, this does not allow us to assume that they were completely illiterate. As this quote from Leo Africanus points out, books were particularly popular in West Africa at this time.

Timbuktu was one of the most famous cities in the Malian Empire as well as an important commercial trading center. It was also known as one of the great centers of learning in the Islamic world, with scholars studying things like astronomy and mathematics. Timbuktu was originally a small trading post near the Niger River. As the Trans-Sahara trade began to develop, Timbuktu became a prosperous trading center. Education was also highly valued, and the city contained several universities and hundreds of schools. One university in particular was the University of Sankore, which was constructed around 1325 during the reign Mansa Kankan Musa. During the time of the Malian Empire, the University of Sankore had one of the highest levels of learning in the entire Islamic world. At its height, the university housed as many as twenty-five thousand students and over four hundred thousand manuscripts. These universities drew scholars from all parts of the earth. Some historians even considered Timbuktu to be one of the greatest learning centers of the Middle Ages. Timbuktu was also one of the few surviving African medieval cities.

According to some historians, the Malian Empire, at its height, was as large as all of Western Europe. Annually, thousands of merchant caravans were counted traveling on each of the several major trade routes that led to various cities in the empire. There were as many as four hundred cities in the entire empire, and parts of the empire were densely inhabited, with many vassals or allied states that acknowledged the emperor's rulership. The emperor maintained a professional army of one hundred thousand men, along with several thousand camels and horses for cavalry.

Toward the end of the fourteenth century the empire suffered many power struggles. After the death of Mansa

Musa in 1337, he was succeeded by his son Mansa Maghan. Four years later, however, Maghan died, and his uncle Sulayman succeeded him. Unlike his brother Mansa Musa, Mansa Sulayman was unpopular with his subjects. Despite this, Sulayman was an effective ruler and maintained stability in his empire. It was during the reign of Sulayman that the famous Arab traveler Ibn Battuta visited the Malian Empire in 1352.

Sulayman ruled for twenty-four years. He was succeeded by his son Kanba, yet civil war erupted shortly afterward. Apparently the sons of Mansa Musa were determined to retake the throne from Sulayman's descendants. A year later, Mari Jata II, a descendent of Mansa Musa, ascended to the throne in 1360. Mari Jata II was a vicious tyrant who almost ruined the empire with his greed and foolish spending. Luckily for his subjects Mari Jata II fell ill and died in 1373. Mari Jata was succeeded by Mansa Musa II who proved to be nothing like his father. Musa II had a counselor who managed to take control of the government during his reign. Although Musa II's councilor was not the Mansa, he made great efforts to rebuild the empire. He mobilized the Malian army and launched a campaign against the nomadic Sanhaja who had seized control of the empire's copper and salt mines in the north. Mansa Musa was succeeded by Mansa Maghan II, his brother, in 1387. Like his brother, Maghan II was more like a puppet ruler while a more powerful government official was the real ruler. Mansa Maghan II was killed and succeeded by

Sandaki, who was a member of the imperial council. Sandaki was also assassinated and succeeded by Mansa Mahmud who, according to Arab travelers, was the last of the great Mansas.

After decades of off-and-on-again civil wars, the Malian Empire was greatly weakened. In 1433 Mali lost control of Timbuktu. Several more territories were lost to a new rising power, Songhay.

The Songhay Empire

The history of Songhay began long before the decline of the Malian Empire. According to some historians, the history of Songhay began around the eighth century AD. The first major Songhay city was Gao, founded during the ninth century. Gao was a thriving trading center with merchant caravans from as far as Egypt and Morocco. This was also the same time that the Ghanaian Empire, farther west, was at its height of influence. The Songhay Kingdom flourished for several centuries; however, Gao was captured and absorbed into the Malian Empire in 1325. Gao remained an important trading asset to the Malian Empire for the rest of the century. Around 1430, the Malian Empire lost its grip on Gao. (Civil war had critically weakened the Malian Empire's control on distant territories.)

With Gao back under their control, the Songhay established a new dynasty and were on a path of conquest. Under the rule of Sii (King) Ali Beeri, Songhay soon conquered new territory. Ali Beeri was very ambitious and is said to have always been marching his army against invaders and conquering enemies. The Songhay army was both great in number and well-disciplined. Ali Beeri had two main weapons that gave him the advantage during his campaign. First was his cavalry, which proved to be a critical part of his army. His second, and perhaps more unique advantage, was his use of riverboats, which provided him a quicker way to reach his enemies. Also most of the major West African cities were located near rivers, and the use of riverboats provided a quick way to reach them. After defeating his immediate adversaries, Ali Beeri turned his attention to the weakening Malian Empire.

In 1468, Ali Beeri's army marched against Timbuktu. By 1469, Timbuktu was captured; this was a great milestone for Ali Beeri. It was the conquest of Timbuktu that really began the Songhay Empire. The Songhay army then headed west for the city of Djenne. According to some historians, Djenne had become even more important than Timbuktu in terms of trade because of its vast gold mines. The Songhay army was unable to penetrate the city because of its high walls and its defender's fierce resistance. Beeri then decided to besiege the city in an effort to starve the inhabitants into surrender. The siege lasted for several years, but eventually the inhabitants of Djenne agreed to surrender. According to some historians, Ali Beeri was the only ruler to have ever captured Djenne. After the conquest of Djenne, Ali Beeri spent his time defending and administrating his empire. In 1492, Sii Ali Beeri died and was succeeded by his son who only ruled a few months. He was replaced by a stronger leader named Askiya Muhammad.

Askiya Muhammad came to power in 1493; "Askiya" replaced "Sii" as the title for king for all the Songhay kings to follow. Askiya Muhammad is remembered as Muhammad the Great. During his reign Muhammad strengthened and expanded the empire. He also created a professional army. By the sixteenth century, the Songhay Empire was almost the size of the entire European continent[1]. Muhammad also established tributary states in the north. Also during his reign, the capital city of Gao flourished with an inhabitance of as many as one hundred thousand, mainly consisting of merchants. Timbuktu also continued to flourish under Songhay rule, particularly in the fields of trade and scholarship.

Askiya Muhammad was succeeded by his eldest son Musa in 1529, who, right after beginning crowned king, began killing off his rival brothers. In 1531 his surviving brothers joined forces against him and killed him in battle. While the sons of Askiya Muhammad fought over the right to rule the empire, their cousin Muhammad Bonkana seized the throne. Muhammad Bonkana lavished his court with furnishings and courtiers with imported garments. However, Bonkana had Askiya Muhammad, who was still living, imprisoned. He also insulted many of Askiya Muhammad's sacred Muslim traditions.

Consequently, Bonkana was overthrown by Askiya Ismail, a son of Askiya Muhammad. Ismail reined for a little over two years. He then died of natural causes in 1539. Ismail was succeeded by his brother Ishaq. He is remembered as one of most feared and disliked of the Askiya Dynasty. He imposed heavy taxes on merchants, so much so that it almost wrecked the empire's economy. As his enemies grew, Ishaq, fearing betrayal, ordered the execution of anyone he feared might oppose him.

After reining for ten years, Ishaq died, and his brother Dawud, also a son of Askiya Muhammad, succeeded him. Dawud was one of the Songhay Empire's greatest emperors. Under his rein the empire regained stability and prospered. He reorganized the army and led them to victory against the Tuareg nomads in the north. Overall, he was successful in most of his military campaigns. According to some historians, he also established public libraries in the empire. Askiya Dawud reigned for over thirty years in which the empire enjoyed stability and prosperity.

Unfortunately after his death, his sons fought one another for the throne. In 1586 Askiya Muhammad Bani ascended to the throne. It was during his reign that civil war broke out. In the town of Kadara, near Timbuktu, on the Niger River, events took place that sparked a civil war. The town's chief Alu was an oppressive despot. Alu, however, was an officer in the service of Bani. In 1588 Alu imprisoned a man in the service of Muhammad Sadiq, who was a military general. Sadiq responded by killing Alu and then declared a revolt against Bani. Many other military leaders joined him and marched an army against Gao. Bani decided to meet them in battle and marched an army to battle Sadiq. According to historians, Bani was quite overweight and stopped to take a nap during the march. Unfortunately, he was wearing a chain mail cloak during the hottest time of the day and was found dead later that afternoon. Historians believe he may have died due to the heat.

Bani was succeeded by Ishaq II who was determined to remain emperor. Ishaq marched an army against Sadiq who was planning to overthrow him. Ishaq defeated Sadiq and put him to death along with all the other commanders who conspired with Sadiq. The civil war, however, had cost many lives and had severely weakened the Songhay army.

In 1590, Songhay scouts reported that an army for Morocco was headed toward Songhay. The Moroccans were drawn to Songhay by the legends of its immense wealth, particularly gold. The Moroccan army numbered as many as four thousand men (many who were European mercenaries). In order to reach Songhay, the Moroccan army first had to cross the Sahara Desert. This meant that they had to march as many as sixty days through a barren wasteland and blistering hot sun. Despite this natural barrier, the Moroccan army marched through the Sahara headed for Songhay. In 1591 they emerged from the desert having lost as many as a third of their force. However, they had one major advantage: they had gunpowder technology. The Moroccan army was armed with muskets and cannons. These weapons were completely foreign to West Africa at that time.

The Songhay quickly mobilized an army of thirty thousand foot soldiers and cavalry armed with swords, archers, and lances. Despite their numerical advantage, the Songhay soldiers and horses had never heard the deafening sound of cannon and musket fire. This had a deceptive effect on the battle that ensued. Armed with deafening firepower, the Moroccans defeated the Songhay army, which was forced to retreat south. This left the major cities of the empire also undefended, so the Moroccans pillaged and plundered the cities of Gao, Djenne, and Timbuktu. In the process of looting gold, the Moroccans destroyed hundreds of libraries, which resulted in the loss of thousands of books.

After their conquests of the major Songhay cities, the Moroccan general Judar Pasha was replaced by Mahmud Pasha, who had orders to complete the conquest of Songhay. By this time the Songhay army had regrouped and was launching small guerrilla skirmishes against Moroccan occupation. After two years of fighting, Mahmud Pasha was unable to put down the rebellion and returned to Timbuktu. The Songhay continued to fight but never overthrew the Moroccans' iron yoke. The year 1591 marked the end of the Songhay Empire.

Consequently, the fall of the Songhay Empire marked the end of West Africa's golden age. The golden age of West Africa began in the sixth century AD with the rise of Ghana and ended in 1591 with the fall of Songhay. Some historians speculate that the golden age quite possibly began as early as the fifth century AD. During this golden age, West Africa was home to some of the wealthiest men and revered scholars. The West African city of Timbuktu is still remembered because of its great wealth and knowledge. It is also important to point out that the great cities of Gao and Timbuktu are not lost cities and can be found on a modern-day globe. Finally, the golden age of West Africa is another testament to the advanced civilization in Sub-Saharan Africa before the modern age.

Kanem-Bornu

During the golden age of West Africa, other empires were rising in the east in central Sahara. According to many historians, Kanem-Bornu began around the ninth century. Like the empires of Ghana and Mali, much of our knowledge of Kanem-Bornu is attained from Arab writers who visited throughout the centuries. One of these early Arab visitors was Al-Yaqubi who traveled to Kanem-Bornu during the late ninth century AD. According to Al-Yaqubi, Kanem-Bornu had a very humble beginning. Al-Yaqubi observed that people of Kanem-Bornu in the ninth century lived in huts made of corn stalks. They also lived in small towns.

However, one hundred years later, the Arab traveler Al-Muhallabi returned with a much different experience. Al-Muhallabi is believed to have visited Kanem-Bornu in 985AD. According to Al-Muhallabi, Kanem-Bornu had become a powerful and important kingdom in the central Sahara. It was governed by a king who ruled by divine right and had two particularly populous cities. Al-Muhallabi also noted that the buildings were then made of clay (possibly oven-baked clay bricks). According to historians, Al-Muhallabi visited the Zaghawa who had established these mighty cities.

During this time the Zaghawa were a powerful people in

Kanem-Bornu, but they were a warlike people and were often at war with their neighbors. The Zaghawa also engaged in slave trading with the Arabs in Egypt, where they traded slaves for the latest weaponry. These included horses bred in the Barbary Coast. Consequently, the Zaghawa army was armed with the best swords, shields, horses, and lances. This gave them an advantage against their neighbors.

Aside from their military, the Zaghawa people built highly developed city-states with mighty walls. Although the Zaghawa had craftsmen who were skilled in clay and metal working, the majority of the population consisted of subsistent farmers. The Zaghawa had a great cultural influence on the rest of Kanem-Bornu.

During the eleventh century, the Zaghawa, under the rule of King Arku, established their jurisdiction over the Muslims trading in the Northern Sahara. Growing interaction with Muslim merchants led to the conversion of many in the aristocracy of the kingdom. Up to this point, Kanem-Bornu was ruled by the Dugawa Dynasty. However, in 1075 AD, Mai Hume Jilmi took control of the kingdom and founded the Sefuwa Dynasty, which ruled Kanem-Bornu for almost eight centuries. Mai Hume Jilmi's descendants were devoted Muslims who made several pilgrimages to the Muslim holy city of Mecca. They also established many mosques of worship throughout the empire. Islam had a great influence on the nobility in the kingdom; however, it had little influence on the middle and lower classes.

In the thirteenth century, Kanem-Bornu was transformed into an empire under the rein of Dunama II. Dunama commanded an army of as many as thirty thousand cavalry mounted camels (for desert warfare) and tens of thousands of foot soldiers. He expanded the empire's power both in the north in modern day Libya and in the south in modern day Nigeria. The Kanem-Bornu cavalry wore quilted armor, which was excellent for fighting in the desert heat. By 1240 the Kanem-Bornu Empire had control over the major trade routes in the region. By the thirteenth century, Kanem-Bornu was well-acquainted with the Eastern world, and they had established trade relations with the many North African nation states. Their trade routes were protected by fortified garrisons.

Under the rule of Dunama II, the Kanem-Bornu Empire thrived. However, there was some internal trouble. Dunama II was a devout Muslim, and he converted many of the conquered peoples. His religious zeal drove him to attempt to destroy traditional religions still practiced by many in the empire, and his fierce opposition against the traditional religions threatened the stability of the empire. A newly conquered territory called Bulala rebelled against Dunama II to avenge the insult against their traditional religion. Some of Dunama II's subjects also joined the rebellion, including some of his own sons. Dunama II successfully put down the rebellion and established an empire that prospered for centuries.

In 1465 Ali Ghaji ascended to the throne. Ail Ghaji was responsible for many governmental, military, and religious reforms. First, he established a new capital, Ngazargamu, in 1484. Ngazargamu was an elaborate city with many large and complex brick buildings and palaces. Gold was plentiful in the empire during this time. An Arab historian, Leo Africanus, visited the empire during the sixteenth century. He later wrote that the emperor's cavalry had gold buckles and stirrups and that even the emperor's royal dogs had chains made of gold. Also, according to some historians, Kanem-Bornu was found on a Portuguese map made in 1489; thus, news of Kanem-Bornu's great wealth had reached even Europe.

In 1564 Mai Idris Alooma ascended to the throne. Alooma gained substantial prestige throughout North Africa. According to some historians, Alooma's armies were possibly one of the first Sub-Saharan armies to be armed with muskets. This gunpowder weaponry was probably obtained through trade with the Turkish merchants. Alooma also encouraged more learning throughout the empire. Also during the reign of Alooma, the Songhay Empire fell in 1591. This gave Kanem-Bornu a monopoly over the Trans-Sahara trade. Mai Idris Alooma was probably one of Kanem-Bornu's greatest rulers.

The Kanem-Bornu Empire continued to prosper into the seventeenth century. The Imperial army continued to successfully repel invasions on all its borders. In 1658 the capital city of Ngazargamu had a population of as many as two hundred fifty thousand, and architecture had become very sophisticated. Many of the streets in the city were unbending, which suggests a level of city planning.

This prosperity was challenged in 1667 by two invasion attempts. From the north in the Sahara Desert came the Tuareg nomads, who were camel raiders. The Tuareg raiders, however, were soon repulsed by Mai Ali of Kanem-Bornu. From the eastern Nigerian territory came the Junkun who raided Ngazargamu as well in search of plunder. Mai Ali also repelled the Junkun.

The empire successfully repelled both invasions, but shortly afterward, a great famine occurred. This was the first of several famines to come, and these continual famines took a great toll on the empire's stability. As the empire weakened, the Tuareg later returned and seized control of the much-needed salt mines. They also interrupted the trade routes, which worsened the famine in parts of the empire. In 1808 a powerful people called the Fulanis occupied Ngazargamu. However, in 1812 they destroyed the city of Ngazargamu, which led to the collapse of the Kanem-Bornu Empire.

The Kanem-Bornu Empire lasted from 1240 to 1812 and

was ruled for the most part by the same dynasty. The Sefuwa Dynasty lasted almost six centuries, making it one of the longest dynasties in world history. Kanem-Bornu was famous all throughout the Oriental world and even in Europe as an empire of great power and wealth. The Kanem-Bornu civilization was one of the most advanced African civilizations both socially and militarily. Like the other West African empires, Kanem-Bornu was highly developed in science, mathematics, and commerce. However, unlike Ghana, Mali, or Songhay, the empire of Kanem-Bornu was successful in attaining cutting-edge military technology, such as gunpowder weaponry. This insured the survival of the empire and made it one of the longest lasting Sub-Saharan empires in African history.

The Asante Empire

The last West African empire we will discuss is the Asante Empire located in the Gold Coast in the modern day nation of Ghana. Historians do not fully know the origins of the Asante people. Some historians believe that they might have been descendants of the Akan peoples who founded the ancient kingdom of Ghana in the north. After the fall of Ancient Ghana in the thirteenth century, many Akan peoples migrated south to the West African coast. The rise of the Asante Empire occurred a little more than a century after the fall of the Songhay Empire. At its height the Asante Empire was the most powerful kingdom on the Gold Coast.

Before the eighteenth century, the Asante made up several small chiefdoms and were tributary states of the Denkyira Kingdom. In 1701 the Asante chiefdoms were united by Osei Tutu through conquest. To establish his rule over the Asante chiefdoms, Osei Tutu had an Asante priest forge the Golden Stool, which was a sign of national unity. The Asante believed that this stool contained the heart and soul of the nation.

With the Asante united under him, Osei Tutu led them against their former ruler, the Denkyira. At this time the Denkyira was a major power in the Gold Coast; however, the Asante had one advantage: firearms. The Asante acquired firearms from the Dutch who believed the Denkyira were preventing them from trading with other tribes north of the coast. With the use of firearms, the Asante conquered the Denkyira and established themselves as an independent nation.

The conquest of the Denkyira Kingdom greatly enriched the Asante Kingdom. With the fall of the Denkyira, the Asante now had access to the coast, which gave them better access to the Dutch traders. Also with the conquest of Denkyira, the Asante captured the rich gold mines in the territory. With this gold the Asante purchased more guns for their army. Guns were one of the most important items to the Asante. It is important to point out that most West African kingdoms did not have access to firearms, which gave the Asante a decisive edge in their conquests. Armed with guns, the Asante army conquered as many as twenty kingdoms and formed an empire.

Osei Tutu died in 1719 and was succeeded by Opoku Ware. During the rule of Opoku Ware, the Asante Empire reached its greatest extent. In 1766 the British governor of the trading company in the Cape Coast, John Hippisley, wrote that Opoku Ware was "the wisest and most valiant man of his time in West Africa."

The Asante successfully established an empire, but it was wise and skillful governing that held the empire together.

Although the Asante could amass a large and powerful army, they did not have professional soldiers. The Asante army consisted of part-time soldiers who would fight for a particular campaign and then return home. In other words, the Asante army was more like a large militia force. Consequently, the Asante did not have the military power to forcefully maintain peace.

Thus, the Asante emperors used cunning rulership as well as an occasional show of power to maintain their control in the empire, which consisted of as many as forty tributary kingdoms. The Asante emperor, Osei Kwadwo, had a policy of giving gifts to the loyal kings in the tributary states. However, these "gifts" were actually nothing more than a small portion of the annual tribute that the Asante received from these same tributary states. Basically, the loyal kingdoms were given tax refunds. The Asante emperor also had a spy network that provided him with valuable information.

Kumase was the capital city of the Asante Empire. Kumase had a population of around forty thousand to fifty thousand. There were two main societal classes in the Asante Empire. The first class was the nobility, and the second consisted of the middle and lower classes, which were grouped together and considered simply the lesser class. The Asante also had slaves. However, slavery in the Asante Empire was quite different from the slavery that was practiced in the American continents. First of all,

Asante slaves were mainly prisoners of war. Slaves were not a main economic resource, and as a result, there was not a great demand for them. Slaves in the Asante Empire had the right to legally marry and have children that were born free. The abuse of Asante slaves was considered inhuman and was looked down upon in Asante society.[3]

Some historians consider the Asante army to be one of the best African armies of the time. The Asante army is believed to have been able to mobilize as many as two hundred thousand soldiers. An Asante soldier was mainly armed with a musket and a knife. The Asante army's success against its enemies (such as the Fante Kingdom) was due not only to their use of guns but also to their mastery of organization, discipline, and the bravery of their soldiers.

The Asante were also great military tacticians. In battle, the Asante army would send a couple thousand scouts who would advance far ahead of the main army. The scouts then engaged the enemy forces in a small skirmish, mainly to reveal the enemy position. Asante scouts were typically skilled hunters and sniped at enemy forces while hidden behind trees or bushes. Once the enemy position was revealed, the scouts retreated as the main army advanced toward the enemy.

The main army marched in three long lines. When in range the front line unleashed a deadly volley, after which the second line advanced in front of the first line and also fired. They were then followed by the third line, which advanced ahead of the previous two lines and delivered their volley. The third line was then followed by the first line who would deliver their second volley. This tactic was continued until the enemy was destroyed.

This form of attack was very disciplined; each line maintained its organization even when under heavy fire. This discipline was partly due to a special unit of soldiers called the Afonasoate. The Afonasoate were armed with swords and whips. They were positioned behind the rest of the army and flogged or slashed anyone who tried to desert. No one was permitted to flee. Now, that might sound like a barbaric practice; however, at that time, most armies around the world had similar ways of dealing with deserters.

By the nineteenth century, the power of the Asante Empire was felt all throughout the Gold Coast. Soon the Asante encountered the British Empire, which had established a colony along the coast. In 1817 a British expedition was sent to the Asante capital city of Kumase led by Thomas Bowdich. The British visitors were astounded by the immense wealth and size of Kumase. The Asante emperor, Osei Bonsu, greeted the British visitors warmly. However, Bowdich had a difficult time trying to convince Osei Bonsu that the British motives were nothing more than to share with them the benefits of Western civilization. Bowdich was later astonished when an Asante prince asked him, "If the British were so generous, why had they been so different in India?" This, of course, points out that the Asante were not as uninformed about world events as the British had assumed.

Bowdich successfully signed a treaty between the Asante and the British.
However, the British failed to ratify the treaty in 1822, and the dark cloud of war was seen on the horizon. The new British governor, Sir Charles MacCarthy, feared the power of the Asante. Within months, MacCarthy severed all peace relations with the Asante and began mobilizing an army.

Fighting broke out after an African soldier (in service of the British) was executed by the Asante because he had verbally insulted the Asante emperor. The British responded by sending a group of British soldiers to attack the village where the African soldier had been executed. For some reason, their guide led them into an ambush, and the British suffered as many as fifty casualties. After the brief armed conflict, Osei Bonsu appealed for peace and offered to settle their differences. MacCarthy, however, refused and marched his army north to invade the Asante Kingdom.

In 1823 an Asante army was mobilized and marched south to meet the British. MacCarthy then divided his forces into two groups and advanced toward the Asante. However, MacCarthy's two forces were separated as they advanced.

MacCarthy then led an even smaller force of only five hundred men right into the Asante army. He was far ahead of his main army and with little ammunition. The only thing separating MacCarthy's unit from the Asante was a river around sixty feet wide. At first the British successfully repelled the Asante advance. However, the British were soon low on ammunition. As the British volleys began to subside, the Asante were able to cut down trees and quickly erect a bridge across the river. The Asante army then charged across the bridge and destroyed MacCarthy's forces. Almost all of MacCarthy's unit was either killed or captured, and Governor MacCarthy was among the dead. A couple of weeks later, the remainder of MacCarthy's army clashed with the Asante. However, the battle ended as a stalemate, and the British retreated to the coast.

After this point, the Asante fought several wars with the British. As the years progressed, the British slowly began to gain the advantage. One of the main reasons for this was that the British continued to advance in military technology. British soldiers soon fought with repeating rifles and machine guns. British artillery was especially devastating. The Asante, however, continued to fight with outdated muskets that often jammed.

As the years progressed, the technological distance between the two nations grew farther and farther apart. British artillery blew gaping holes in advancing Asante lines. British rifles outranged the Asante musket, which resulted in the Asante suffering hundreds of casualties before they could advance close enough to fire. Despite these disadvantages, the Asante fought with unwavering bravery and amazing discipline. By 1870 the British prepared to invade the Asante Empire. Under the command of General Garnet Wolseley, twenty-five hundred British soldiers, along with several thousand native troops, marched against the Asante in 1873. After two major battles with the Asante forces, the British captured Kumase and burned it to the ground. The British soon withdrew from Asante territory due to disease.

With the destruction of Kumase, Asante power in the Gold Coast was shattered. The Asante Empire lingered on for another twenty years. However, in 1894, after the Asante refused to give up their sovereignty and become a British territory, British forces invaded a second time. Hoping to prevent the French from seizing the Asante's' vast gold mines, the British hastily crushed all resistance. This marked the end of the Asante Empire but not the Asante people. Although they had lost their capital city and most of their power, it was the Golden Stool (which was used by Osei Tutu to unite the Asante in the founding of the empire) that united the people, and as long as the stool was in their possession, they continued to resist British rule for several more years.

The legacy of the Asante Empire is the cunning of their emperors, the discipline of their armies, and the unity of their people. Today many people remember the Zulu nation and how its warriors defended British forces in the Isandlwana but in the end lost the war. The Asante, however, were one of the few nations of people to defeat a European colonial power in a war. Even the British soldiers came to respect the Asante for their bravery and discipline.

(Great Zimbabwe, a medieval ruined city in Zimbabwe)

Chapter 4: South Africa

The Munhumutapa Empire

The first empire to rise in South Africa was the Munhumutapa Empire around the eleventh and twelfth centuries. The Munhumutapa Empire is believed to have been established by the Shona peoples in modern day Zimbabwe. According to oral tradition, in 1085 the Prince of Great Zimbabwe, Mutota, conquered several neighboring tribes to establish control over salt deposits in the region. Salt was of great worth. The empire continued to expand under the leadership of Mutota's successor, Matope. The Mutapa (king/emperor) could mobilize an army numbering as many as one hundred thousand men, which was the standard size of most armies at that time. The capital of the empire was Zimbabwe. The ruins of Great Zimbabwe are some of the oldest remaining structures in Southern Africa today. In the fourteenth century AD, the population of Great Zimbabwe was around eighteen thousand.

Like the empires of Mali and Ghana, Munhumutapa controlled much of the commerce in the region. The Munhumutapa Empire was involved in a trading network that reached as far as Asia. Merchants from the Swahili city-states sailed inland to exchange goods with the Shona merchants. The Swahili merchants exchanged rare goods that had been acquired through trade in the Indian Ocean. Merchants from Munhumutapa traveled to the Swahili city of Sofala. The Shona exported gold, ivory, and copper in exchange for porcelain from China and textiles from India.

Portuguese explorers reached the Munhumutapa Empire for the first time in 1499. They soon established trade relations with one another; however, in 1561 a Jesuit missionary travel to Munhumutapa with the intention of converting the Mutapa to Christianity. Within a month, the missionary had successfully converted and baptized the Mutapa. After the conversion of the Mutapa, the missionary successfully converted many of the high-ranking officials. However, Islamic merchants were greatly alarmed by the missionary's influence. A few days later, the missionary was killed.

News of the missionary's death outraged the Portuguese. The king of Portugal appointed Francisco Barreto to lead an invasion of Munhumutapa. In 1571, the Portuguese invasion fleet arrived at a coastal city name Sena. From there they marched their way to Munhumutapa. On the way, Barreto defeated the kingdom of Samungazi. After the conquest of Samungazi, Mutapa Negomo sent an envoy to the Portuguese to discuss peace terms. Mutapa Negomo agreed to Barreto's demands, which included control over the gold mines in the region. After the peace agreement, the Portuguese returned to Sena and vented their anger on the populace, massacring hundreds.

In 1573, Barreto died (probably from disease) and was replaced by Vasco Homem. Under Homem, the Portuguese remobilized and attacked the Munhumutapa Empire's neighbors. They conquered several kingdoms before Mutapa Negomo responded by sending a vast army of one hundred thousand men to engage Homem in battle. Homem's army, numbering only a couple thousand men, was forced to withdraw in 1577.

Shortly after the war, the Munhumutapa Empire began to decline in power. Munhumutapa also suffered civil war, which led to Portuguese intervention. During the civil war, kingdom after kingdom seceded from the empire. The last true Mutapa was Kapararidze. During his reign, his rival Mavhura began to seek help from the Portuguese in order to take the throne. When Kapararidze discovered the plot, he had the Portuguese diplomat executed. As a result, the Portuguese declared war against Kapararidze. Mavhura, along with others, joined the Portuguese and marched against the capital city. Kapararidze's army was defeated and forced to withdraw. Mavhura was then installed as emperor by the Portuguese in 1629 and made a vassal state of Portugal. This marked the end of the Munhumutapa Empire.

Epilogue:
The Legacy of African Civilization

As we can see, Africa is rich in history. For over four thousand years, civilization has flourished in Africa. From the birth of Egypt around 2700 BC to the rise of the Asante Empire in the late eighteenth century, African civilizations rose to great power and influence.

Ancient Egypt was among the first great civilizations in human history. For centuries the power and influence of Egypt was felt all over the Middle East. The power of Egypt was so great that although Ancient Egypt has passed into history, land is named after it. The Pyramids of Giza are the only remaining wonders of the ancient world and are a testament to the Egyptians' critical understanding of architecture and mathematics. But perhaps one of the most amazing aspects of Ancient Egypt is how advanced it was in comparison to the rest of the world. While Rome was still just a small city, the Egyptian Empire ruled lands as distant as Syria and Kush. While the Greeks were still a cluster of warring city-states, Egypt flourished in mathematics, philosophy, and science. A thousand years before the Chinese built the Great Wall of China the Egyptians built over a hundred pyramids. Egypt was truly one of the greatest civilizations the world has ever known.

The Kushites have a history of greatness and determination. For centuries the Egyptians attempted to conquer the Kushites but were never able to fully subdue them. The Kushites later conquered and ruled Egypt under the leadership of King Taharka. As years progressed, Kush lost control of Egypt to invaders but successfully defended its homeland from invasion. Neither the Persians nor the Greeks nor even the Romans were able to conquer Kush. The Kushites, like the Egyptians, were pyramid builders and actually built more pyramids than the Egyptians.

The nation of Carthage was one of the wealthiest nations in the Mediterranean world. Carthaginian merchant vessels traded with kingdoms from all over the world from as far north as Britain and as far south as Southern Africa. The Carthaginian navy was feared throughout the Mediterranean Sea. Carthage was also the home of one of the world's greatest generals, Hannibal. It was Hannibal's brilliant battle strategies that led him to win most of his battles against the Roman legions. Carthage was the first world power in the Mediterranean world and one of the Roman Empire's most powerful adversaries.

Many historians believe that Moorish Spain brought Western civilization to Europe. Moorish Spain was a place of great learning. When most of Europe was in an age of darkness, Moorish Spain was in an age of knowledge. In Moorish Spain, Jews, Christians, and Moslems lived together in peace. Moorish Spain was truly a light in the midst of a dark age.

The Ethiopian kingdom of Axum was the greatest Christian kingdom in all of Africa. The Ethiopians built several cathedrals and churches. Some of these churches were carved out of solid stone. Axum resisted Islamic invasion for almost a thousand years. In later years Ethiopia was the only African nation to successfully resist Western invasion. Today Ethiopia is a symbol of freedom for the rest of Africa.

The Nubian kingdoms are remembered for their valiant resistance against Arab invasion. For centuries, the Nubians successfully repelled Islamic conquests. The Nubian archers, who rarely missed, were arguably the greatest archers the world has ever seen.

The Swahili city-states played an important role in commerce in the Indian Ocean. The Swahili were masters of iron smelting. As a matter of fact, their quality of iron was unmatched until the nineteenth century. The Swahili were also skilled navigators who sailed on the Indian Ocean to destinations as far as China.

The kings of the West African empires of Ghana, Mali, and Songhay were believed to have been the richest men on the face of the earth during their time. This wealth was mainly acquired through a monopoly of the Trans-Saharan trading sites. When the caravan of the Malian king, Mansa Musa, stopped in Egypt, he spent so much gold that the value of gold plummeted. Ghana, Mali, and Songhay were also remembered for their great love for learning. Scholars from all over the Islamic world traveled to Timbuktu to study in the city's libraries. According to Arab travelers, Timbuktu had doctors and scribes as well as a great number of other men of learning. Although they did not have a native written language, the people of Timbuktu had books written in Arabic. In 1311 AD the Malian emperor sent a fleet on an expedition to sail to the extremity of the Atlantic Ocean. There is a great possibility that the Malians discovered the Americas 181 years before Columbus sailed to the West Indies in 1492. The rise of these three empires marked the golden age in West African history.

The Asante Empire was one of the last African kingdoms to fall to colonial invasion. For a hundred years, the Asante fought to maintain their independence. The Asante nobility were well-educated. Among the treasures in the emperor's palace was his personal library. The Asante were one of the few African nations to win a war against the European colonial powers. Their success can be attributed to the discipline of their army and the bravery of their soldiers. The Asante are remembered for their long and fierce resistance even after their empire had been destroyed. As long as the Golden Stool was in their hands, they resisted British rule.

All over Africa there are ruins of great civilizations. The

nations such as Egypt, Carthage, Moorish Spain, and Mali are known throughout the world. People still think of Africa as a continent of just natural wonders. Yet, as we can see, like every other continent in the world, Africa is a place of civilization and human progress. From as early as 2700 BC, Africans built densely populated cities, lavish palaces, and formidable fortresses. Many African nations studied science, mathematics, history, and even writing.

Now some might ask, "What is so important about African history?" The answer to this question is that African history is part of world history, and in order to better understand our world today, we must first understand every aspect of world history. In the world today, there are many theories advocating racial inferiority. It is believed by some that black people are good at basketball and other physical activities but generally lack the mental capacity to excel in brain-demanding matters. Some black people even believe that pursuing an education and speaking articulately is "acting white." However, when we take a look at African history, we find that people of African descent founded mathematics and philosophy. They excelled in both physical and mental activities and their modern descendants can do the same. Today many people study history from only one perspective—the European perspective. But this is incomplete; Europe is only a small fraction of the world. When Europe was in the Middle Ages, advanced civilizations flourished in many other areas around the globe. So, as it is now obvious to see, Africa has played a critical role in world history.

Bibliography

1. When We Ruled by Robin Walker
2. Lost Cities of Africa by Basil Davidson
3. The Fall of the Asante Empire by Robert B. Edgerton
4. Empires of Medieval West Africa by David C. Conrad
5. Library of Nations: East Africa by Time-Life Books
6. The Civilizations of African by Christopher Ehret
7. World Geography in Christian Perspective Grade 9 (A Beka Book) by Brian Ashbaugh
8. Conflict in the 20th Century: Africa from 1945 by Dr. Simon Baynham
9. The Splendor that was Africa by Ricky Rosenthal
10. Ethiopia in the Modern World by John G. Hall
11. Ancient Africa by John Addison
12. East Africa by Lawrence Fellows
13. Cradles of Civilization: Egypt by Jaromir Malek

Printed in Great Britain
by Amazon